I0804293

ARCHITECTURE OF PLACE

BATES MASI + ARCHITECTS

ORO EDITIONS
NOVATO, CA

INTRODUCTION BY PILAR VILADAS

CONTENTS

INTRODUCTION

BY PILAR VILADAS

The title of this book, *The Architecture of Place*, is a particularly apt one. Since its founding, Bates Masi + Architects has remained true to its Modernist roots, designing thoughtfully organized, elegantly detailed houses that are open, warm, and comfortable, with a considered and imaginative approach to materials, and which embody the functional and environmental issues of the present day. These houses, the majority of which are weekend homes on the East End of Long Island, address the needs and wishes of clients and the physical and historical aspects of a site, as well as historical archetypes like the pitched-roof forms of the saltbox houses that are still common in the area. The East Hampton-based firm began as an unlikely but successful partnership between Harry Bates, who was in his 70th year, and who—after founding his office in 1965, became known for the Modernist houses he designed in the Hamptons and on Fire Island–and Paul Masi, who was then in his 20s and starting out in the profession. Since Bates's retirement, Masi has directed the firm, maintaining his former partner's philosophy of "considering the totality of the project," he says. "It was interesting to talk to Harry about the evolution of second homes on Long Island," Masi recalls. "The houses became more sophisticated, but still addressed the question of how you maintain the essence of an exciting place to live."

Even though the Modernist houses of the 1950s and '60s on Long Island were much more modest, as they were often commissioned by artists, writers, and other creative types, Modernist architecture in this area–despite the rise of much larger, more traditional houses built by much wealthier people in the 1980s and beyond–never really went away. Its revival began in earnest in the 1990s and continues today, although it seems to have split into two camps. One promotes large-scale, obviously expensive dwellings that tend to dominate their surroundings, while the other favors more modestly scaled houses that are an integral part of their settings, and for which luxury is not so much a matter of ostentation, but of proportion, light, and connection to the land.

In many of Bates Masi's projects, this balance also honors the history of the land and its uses, and the historic architecture in the area, in their designs for houses. In other projects, the increasing vulnerability of the land to climate change and sea-level rise is an important factor in the design. While some houses in the area are protected from flooding by strategies like raising them on large stilts, the results can look inorganic. Instead, Bates Masi's designs take these issues and integrate them into the design. For example, their methods include flood-mitigation measures, like elevating and breaking up the forms of the house to let water flow around them, thus lessening the threat of damage from surging waters, but also recognizing flooding as a natural event. A house can also be raised above a flood plain, for example, while its design ensures that it remain an integral part of the landscape.

And sometimes, a client's lifestyle drives the design. A number of Bates Masi's houses consist of separate but connected forms that balance community and privacy, so that three generations of a family can enjoy both community and privacy. For clients who prefer water sports and sailing, the architects design houses that offer ample exposure to sun, breezes, and water.

Materials offer another opportunity for Bates Masi to go beyond the ordinary. For example, the architects used thatch—which is still used for roofs in Europe and the United Kingdom, but which is not a common building material in this country–on the exterior of a house, albeit in a contemporary way, packed between the exposed exterior framing. "Not only does the material grow out here," Masi says, "but it's very similar to shingling, and it's very organic. It's exciting for us to take something and give it a new identity." And while the architects are known for their use of wood, on both the exterior and interior, that use is evolving. Wood panels become oversize shingles, or cedar siding is suspended from bronze rods or stainless-steel clips, so that the boards can expand and contract with changes in the weather. In one house, thin cedar strips of the rainscreen siding were fastened only at the center, allowing the ends to warp naturally, in contrast to the strict lines of the framework. These materials and others, like the steel panels used at the bases of some houses, are chosen for their ability to weather gracefully; making a house look brand-new and shiny forever is not the goal. These architects prefer materials that weather well and take on a beauty of their own, without constant maintenance. And in the interiors of these houses, for example, knotty white oak is wire-brushed to bring out its texture rather than being stained; clay tiles are used like shingles to cover a tall fireplace; and limestone is given varied finishes according to its use—rougher for outdoors, for example, or polished for kitchen countertops, to make it more sanitary.

While a lot of the firm's early work was very expressive in its materials, its more recent work looks at the ways forms can support buildings, as in a design for a house with a curved back that will allow the wind to blow seeds up over the roof and onto the front of the property. The work has long been focused, with a few exceptions, on the East End of Long Island, but as its project portfolio expand to other states and countries, the nature of those places will continue to be a focal point.

And while Bates Masi is constantly exploring new forms of architectural expression, Harry Bates's influence is still very much a part of the firm's philosophy. "The materials could be very ordinary, but Harry would elevate them with details," Masi says, calling the approach "ways to take the everyday and make a more unique experience. That continues in our work. It's something that everyone in our office gets excited about—getting to that level of detail to tell the story, and that's what we all love."

PROMISED LAND

2015

The owners of this Amagansett property and their family have a passion for being on the water. Their interests–wind surfing, kite boarding, and sailing–all depend on the wind and the resulting sea conditions. Whether relaxing at home or on a nearby beach, the owners are constantly searching for cues that conditions are optimal to get on the water. Thus, their home is designed to respond to and register the wind, becoming an instrument by which to gauge and appreciate it.

Site research revealed a remarkable consistency in the westerly wind direction. As a result, the home and site designs are arranged along an east-west axis. Along this axis, a narrow clearing in the forest channels the wind toward a courtyard that separates the public and private wings of the house. A glass-enclosed breezeway bisects the courtyard to connect the two wings, but its walls can be completely opened to allow the wind to flow through the site uninterrupted. Within the courtyard, in parallel with the axis, a reflecting pool acts as a barometer for displaying the status of the wind. Not only do the ripples in the water surface highlight the direction and intensity of the breeze, but sunlight and artificial light reflect off the surface onto the ceiling overhangs above, projecting and amplifying the animated pattern of the waves.

The structural system is comprised of a series of exposed glulam wood beams running east-west with venting panels between each beam at the perimeter. To achieve large spans, the beams are joined by steel flitch plates that create voids within the structure for light fixtures. Flitch plates also cantilever from the ends of the beams to support the thin profile roof that extend from all sides of the house. The overhangs capture the wind, directing it through the venting panels and along the beams to passively ventilate the home at the height of the ceiling, with less disturbance to the living areas below than simply opening the doors.

With the recognition of wind in the architecture comes the opportunity for the landscape to contribute to the experiences of the house. Lavender, mint, and other aromatic plants were introduced to the windward side of the property. As it traverses the site, the wind picks up scents along the way and carries them into the living spaces.

Acting as a tool for highlighting environmental information, the architecture is dependent on the context. However, without the unique interests of its inhabitants this information is less meaningful. Because of their interdependent relationship, both place and lifestyle are enriched in a single gesture.

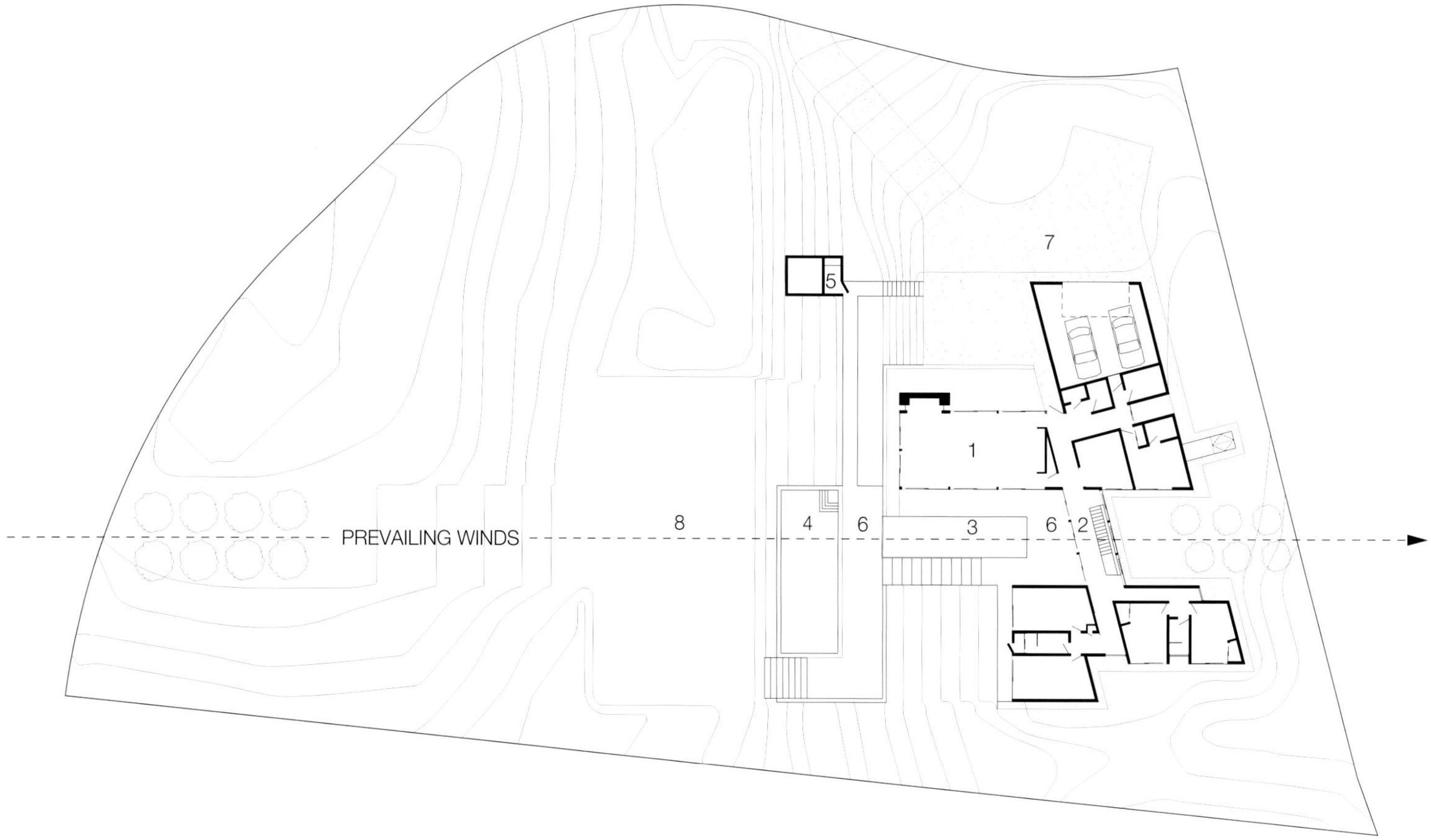

SITE PLAN

1. House
2. Breezeway
3. Reflecting Pool
4. Swimming Pool
5. Outdoor Shower
6. Deck
7. Driveway
8. Lawn

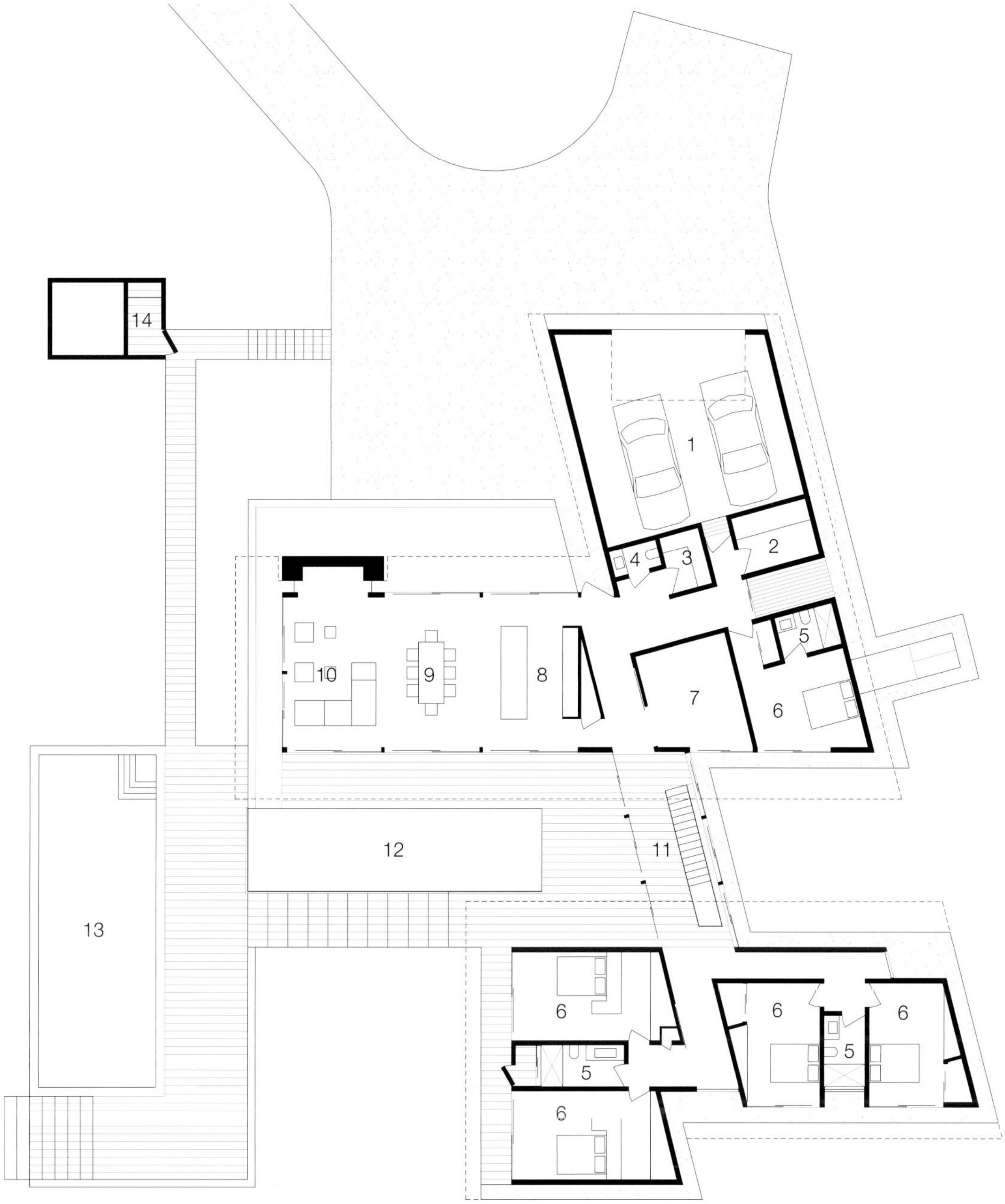

GROUND LEVEL PLAN

1. Garage
2. Laundry
3. Coat Closet
4. Powder Room
5. Bath
6. Bedroom
7. Play Room
8. Kitchen
9. Dining
10. Living
11. Breezeway
12. Reflecting Pool
13. Swimming Pool
14. Outdoor Shower

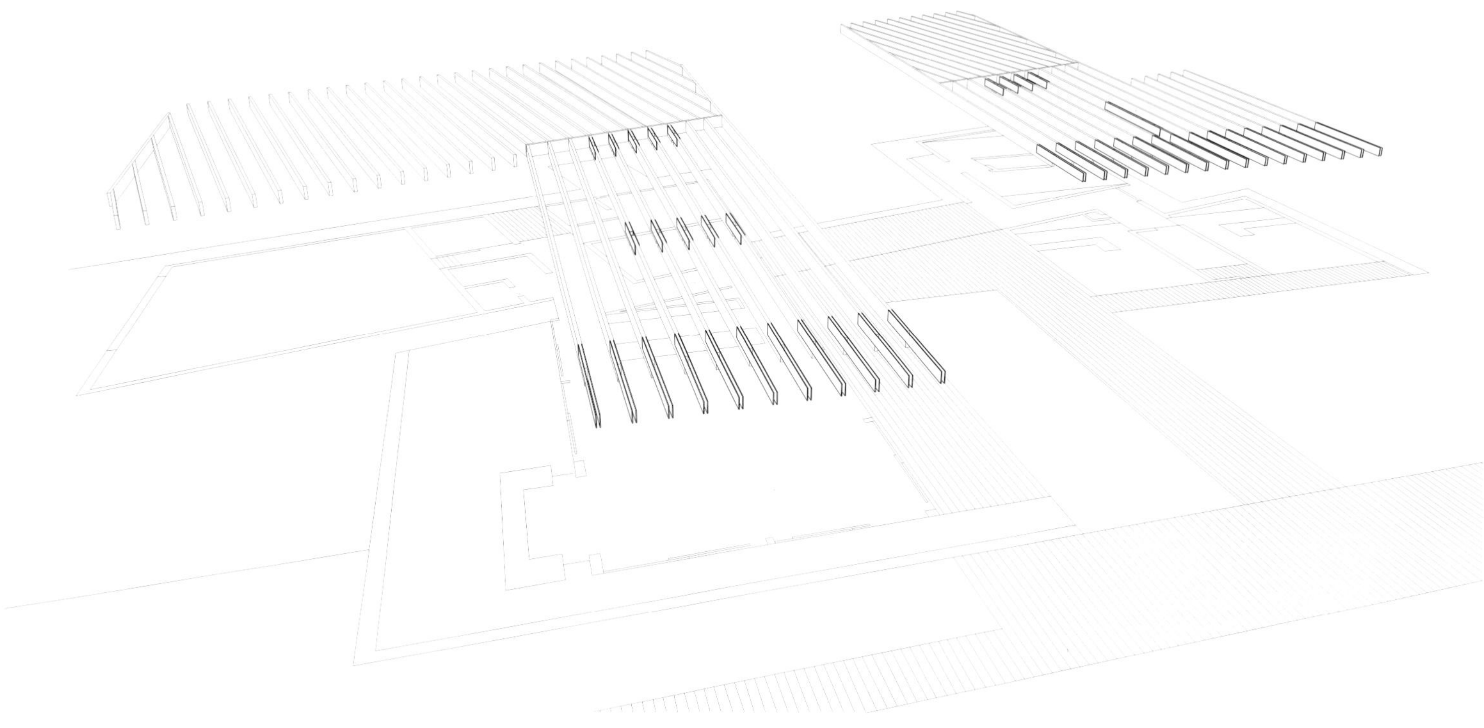

Alignment of structure and predomimant wind direction.

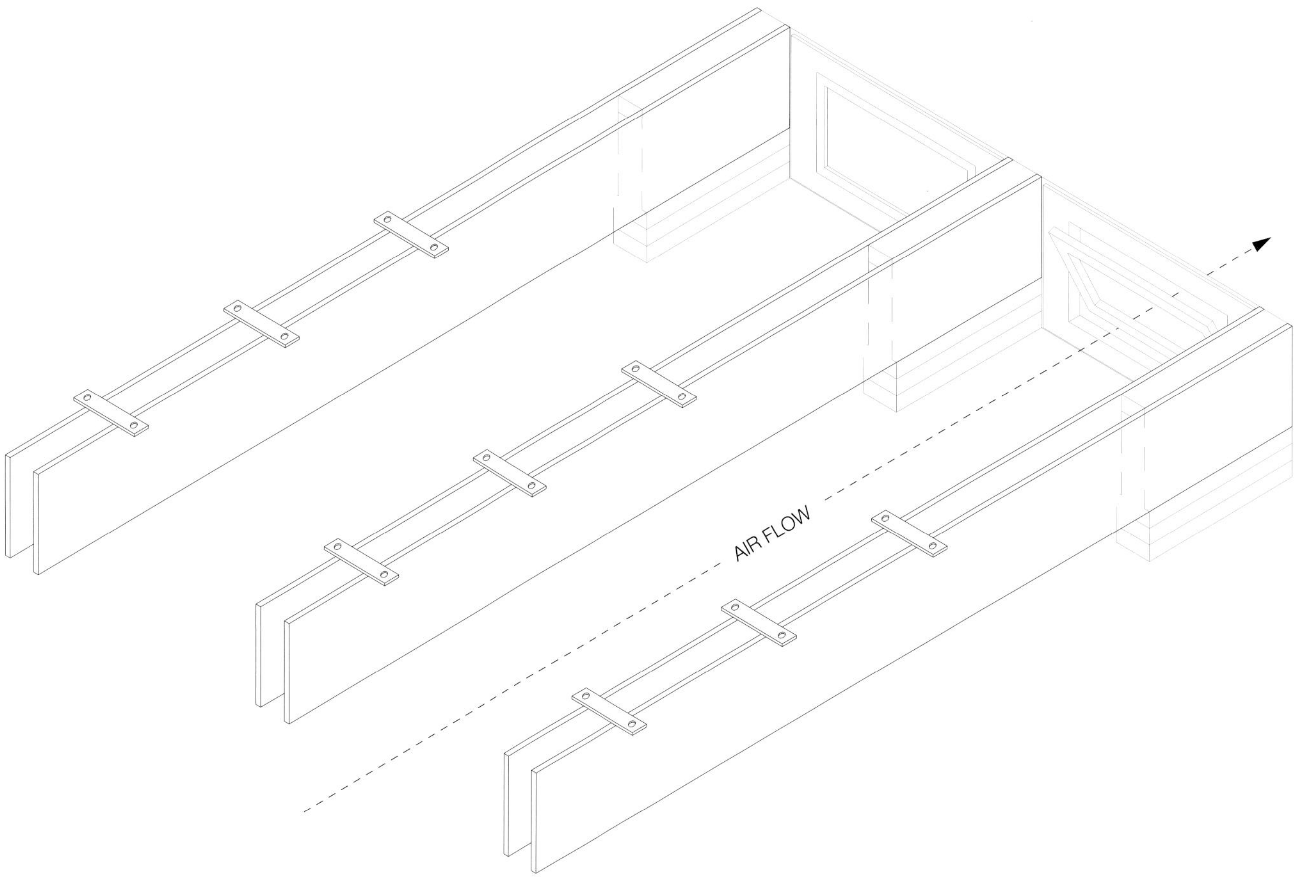

Roof eave detail captures air flow.

Reflecting pool construction sequence.

Adjustable vents within structure.

Aromatic plantings along windward axis.

Wind animates reflected light off the water.

ATLANTIC

2015

Across the street from the property, in the low dunes near the Atlantic Ocean, a historic Life Saving Station serves as a cherished reminder of the maritime, military, and architectural history of this coastal landscape. Built over a century ago, the station is part of a network of structures used to provide rescue and relief for shipwrecked sailors, and it was from this station that a guard once discovered Nazi invaders coming ashore during World War II. Designed with lookout towers, weather-protected cupolas, and elevated decks, the stations offered many views for the crews to survey the horizon through all seasons. Inside, large, open storage rooms often featured boats, oars, and other equipment hung from exposed beams for easy access. Taking cues from this structure, the design of the new residence strikes a dialogue with the landmark to enrich the experience of the new home and celebrate the local history.

The principal strategy for the home stems from the utilitarian practice of hanging boats and other items from the station's wooden post and beam structure. In a modern reinterpretation, the residence features an exposed steel structure that defines the main living spaces and forms a framework onto which other functions can be hung: the main stair is strung from beams above, and the rods used to support each tread serve as guardrail for the stair; a wood-burning stove sits on a suspended steel shelf; light fixtures are fastened to the flanges using standard beam clamps; a swinging chair hangs from the cantilevered living area above.

On the exterior, a system of bronze bars was developed to hang the thick cedar siding boards in place without fastening through the wood, allowing the boards to expand and contract naturally with changes of temperature and humidity. Like the weathered cedar shingles on the Station across the street, each material—cedar, bronze, and weathering steel—was chosen for its proven durability in the coastal climate. As each material weathers over time, the appearance of the siding will record the cycles of rain, sun, freeze, and thaw: cedar will lighten from the sun; bronze bars will patina to dark brown and eventually turn green; weathering steel will develop a deep rusted texture on the surface that protects it from further corrosion by the salty air. The weathering steel around the base of the building marks the height the home was raised above the flood plane. To minimize the impact of the footprint on the sensitive ecological environment, the main living area is stacked above the bedrooms, and, like the lookout towers of the stations, an even higher roof deck provides elevated views of the ocean.

By taking cues from the historic lifesaving station, the home responds to the environmental and historical context. In so doing, it honors the local heritage and enriches the present day experience.

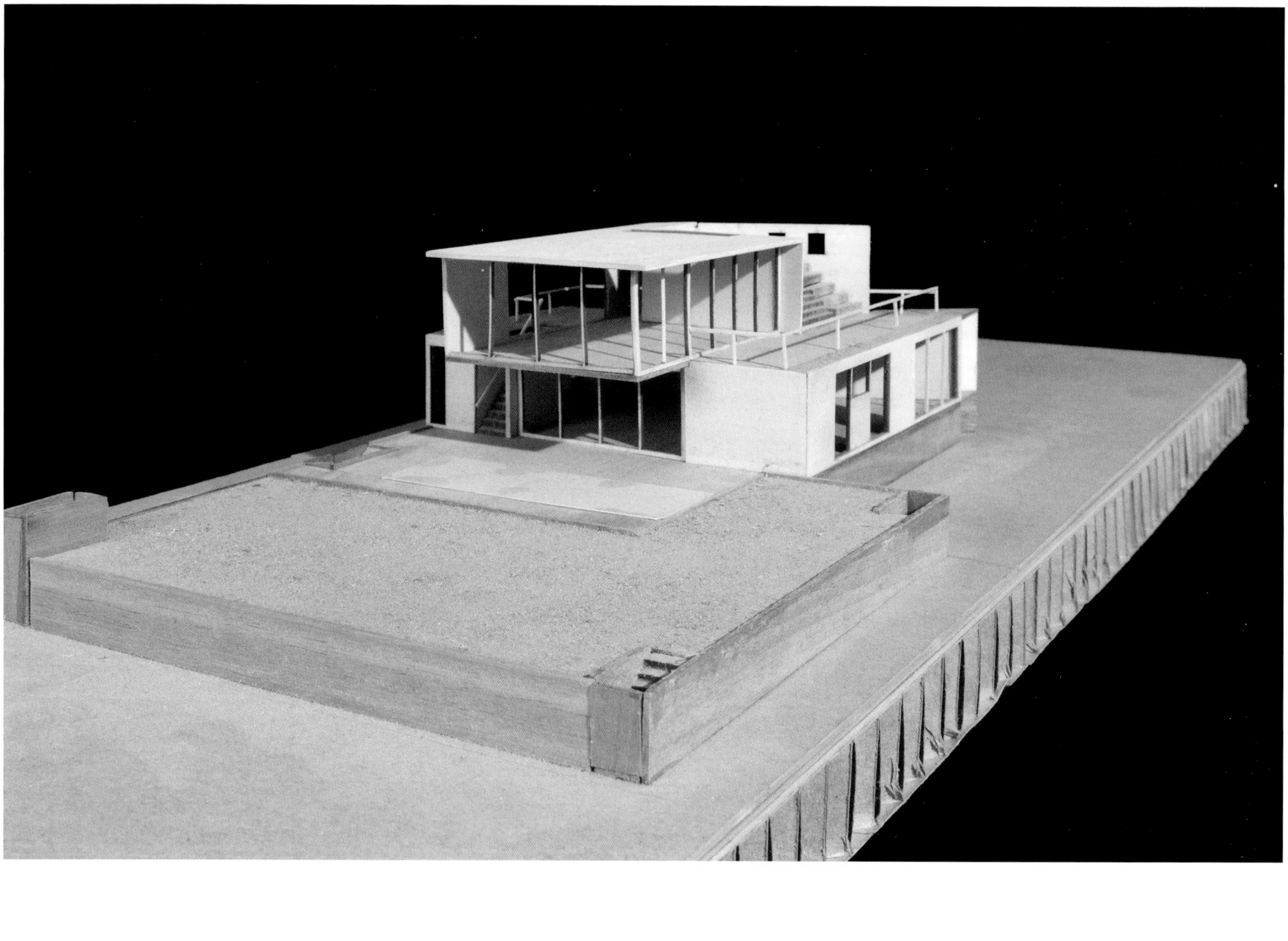

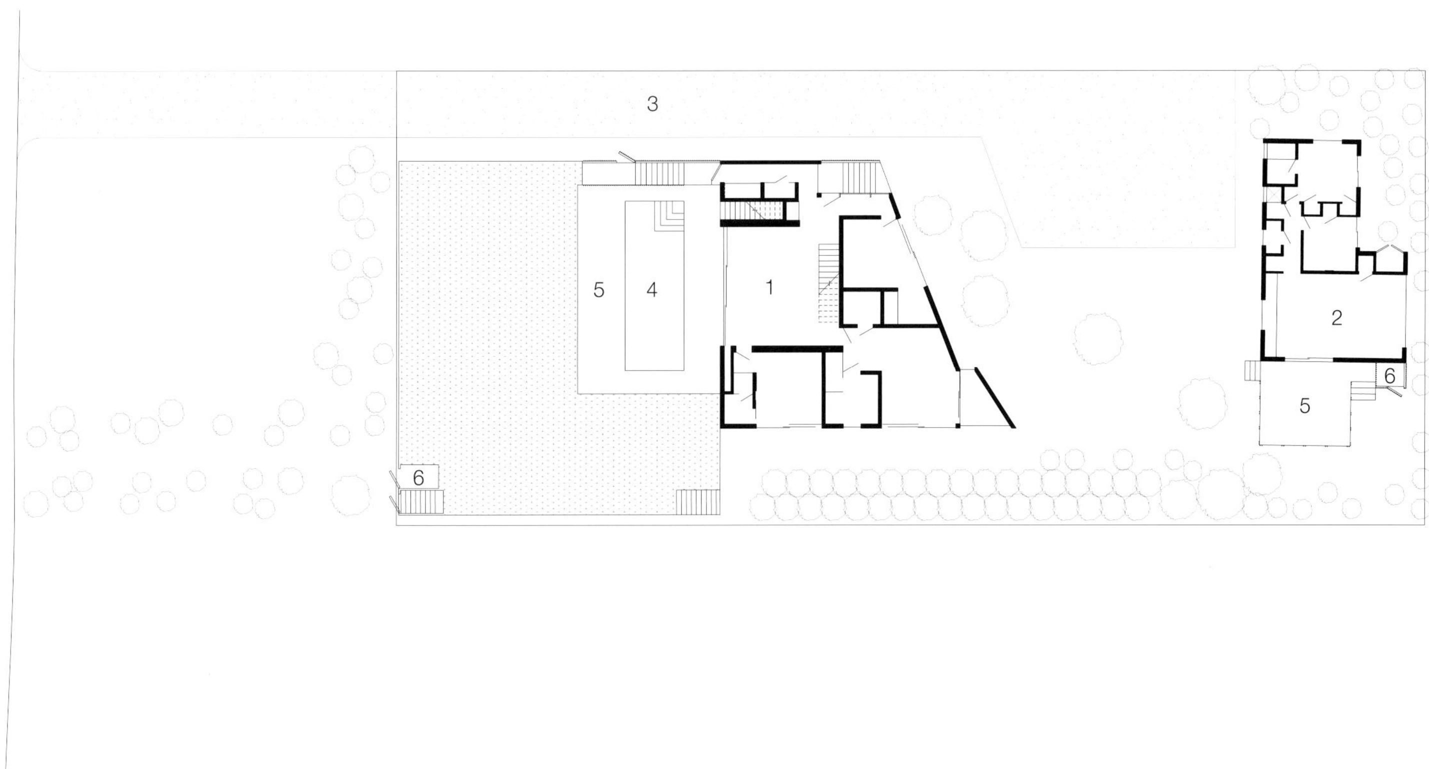

SITE PLAN

1. Main House
2. Cottage
3. Driveway
4. Pool
5. Deck
6. Outdoor Shower

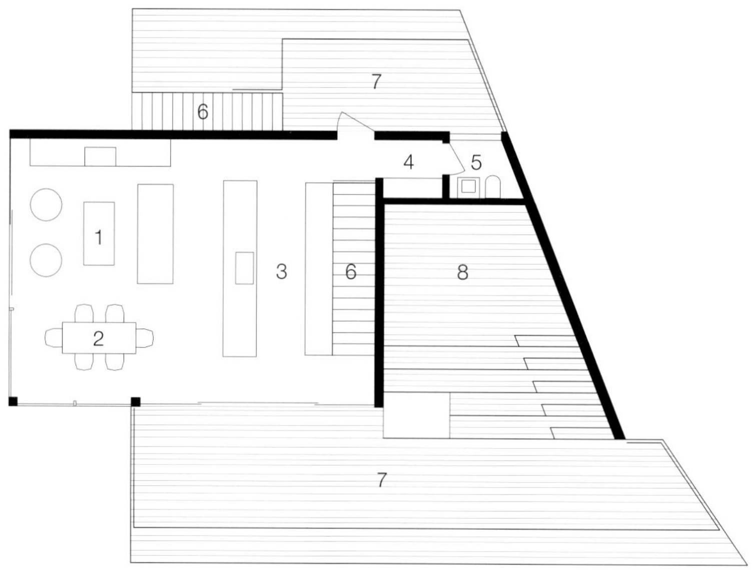

MAIN HOUSE UPPER LEVEL PLAN

1. Living
2. Dining
3. Kitchen
4. Pantry
5. Powder Room
6. Stair
7. Roof Deck
8. Lookout Deck

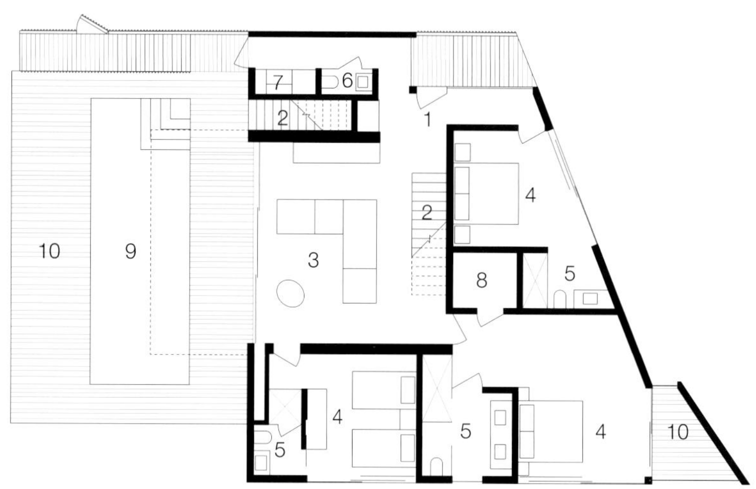

MAIN HOUSE GROUND LEVEL PLAN

1. Entry
2. Stair
3. Family Room
4. Bedroom
5. Bath
6. Powder Room
7. Laundry
8. Mechanical
9. Pool
10. Deck

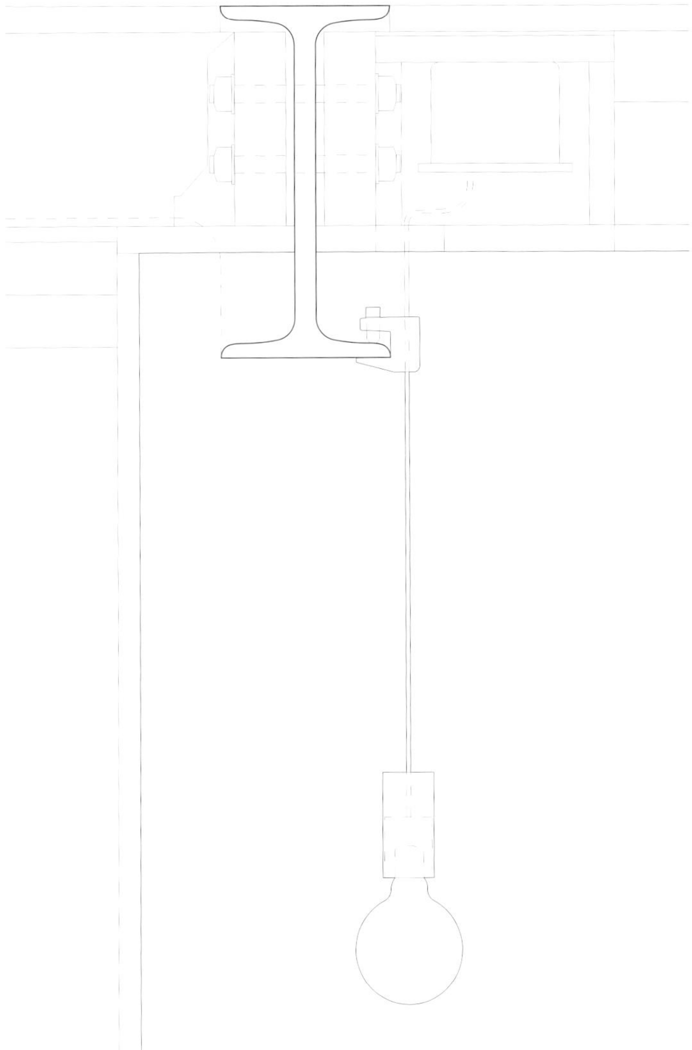

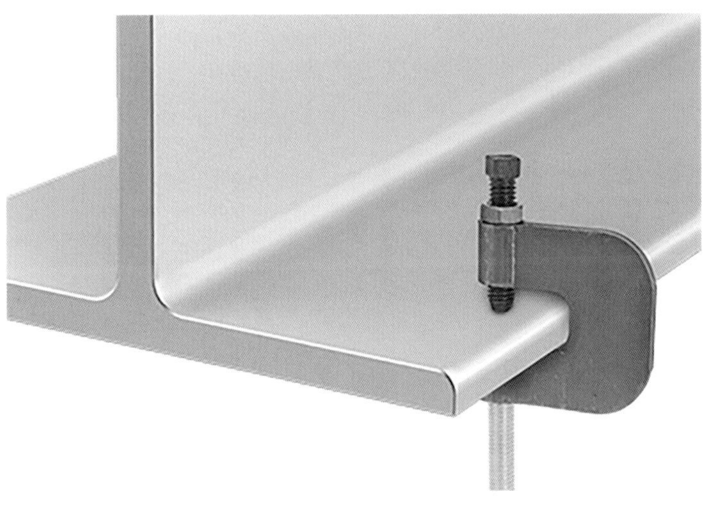

Framework onto which other functions are hung.

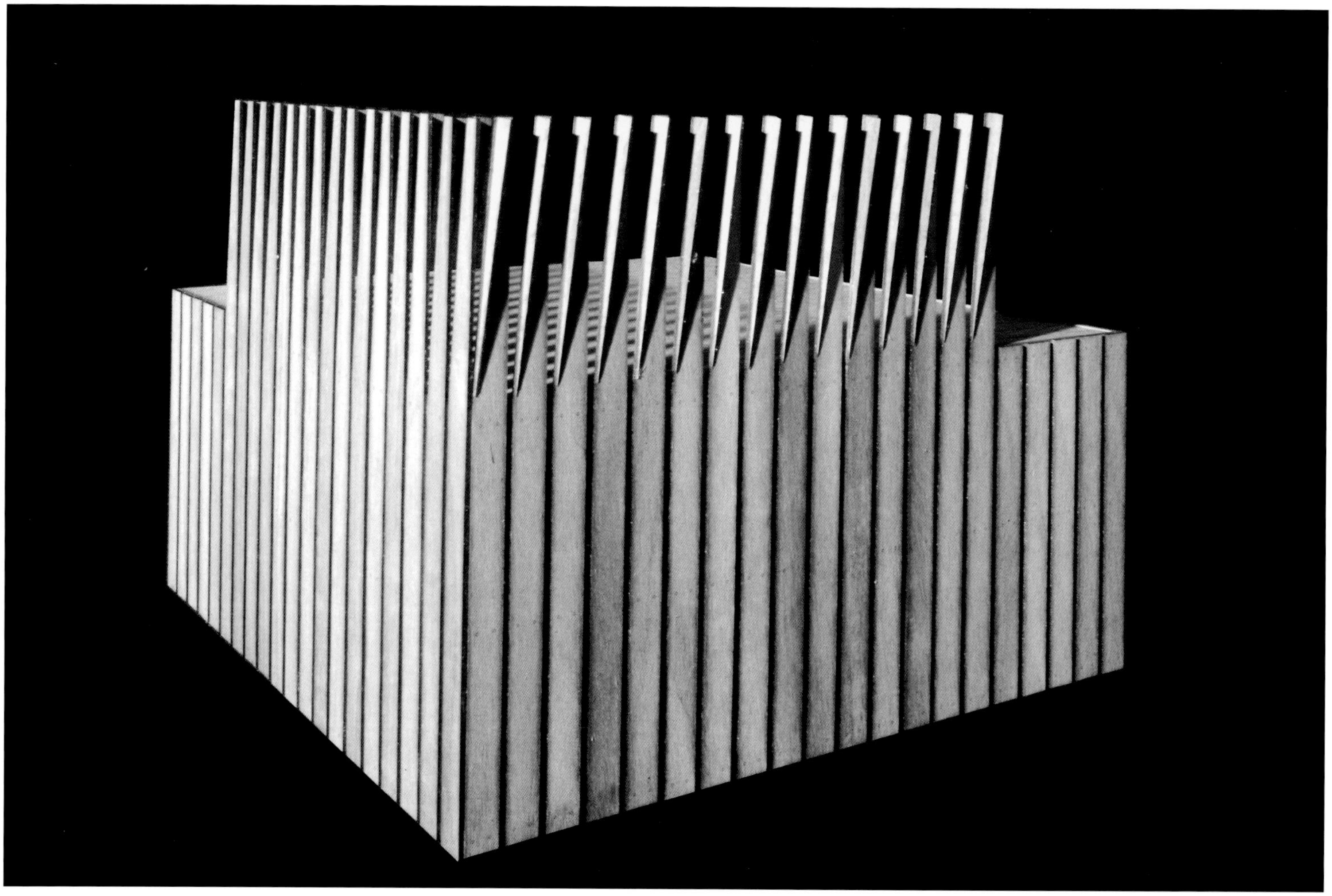

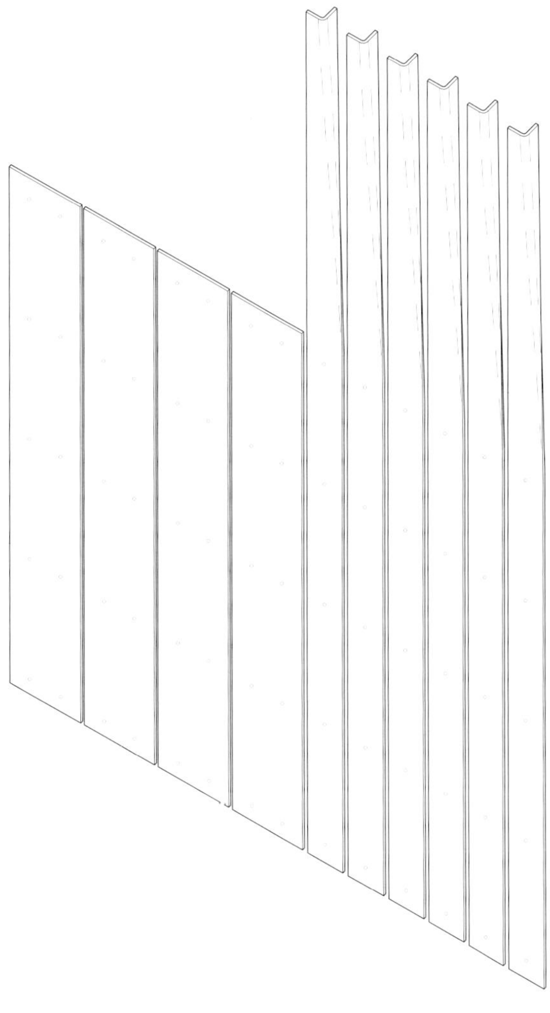

Cladding folded to selectively open views.

Bronze bars hang siding, allowing expansion and contraction.

Lighting, shelving, stair, and furniture hung from structure.

Dialogue with historic lifesaving station.

GEORGICA COVE

2017

A couple with property on a cove overlooking the ocean asked for a house that would be comfortable for just the two of them the majority of the time. However, with their love of entertaining, the house had to grow on busy weekends to accommodate their children, grandchildren, and guests. To instill the desired sense of comfort and peace, it was also important that the design blend with the pastoral setting and vernacular building traditions: predominantly shingle-style homes and barns that are often built and added to over time. Historic precedent studies revealed that referencing New England connected farms in an innovative way could achieve both goals.

Connected farms aggregated over time, interconnecting multiple buildings with distinct uses. The architectural style of the house was applied to subsequent buildings to unify the assembly, but partitions within provided the necessary separation between uses: house to kitchen, kitchen to shop, and shop to barn for instance. One volume was often offset or rotated from the next to provide greater access to light, air, and privacy from the other functions. Following that example, the program of this house is divided into owners' bedroom and office, eat-in kitchen and family room, formal living and dining, and guest rooms. The spaces are arranged around a courtyard to create visual and physical connections between them but those connections can be broken by large sliding doors. Each structure has an independent mechanical system allowing it to be shut down when unoccupied. This allows the livability of the house to expand and contract whether the couple is alone, hosting dinner guests, or has a full house of overnight guests.

As with connected farms, a limited palette of materials and details unifies the various spaces and responds to the local climate. The cedar shingles common to local buildings are scaled up to the size of boards to cover the roof and sidewalls. Cedar screens provide privacy and filter light. A marble plinth filled with sand elevates the house above the floodplain while also creating drywells to accept storm water runoff. Oak floors and millwork throughout unify the spaces.

The design repurposes the historic typology of the connected farm to suit the very timely needs of the site and the family. By acknowledging the area's history and tradition of building, this home is an evolution of its cultural expression.

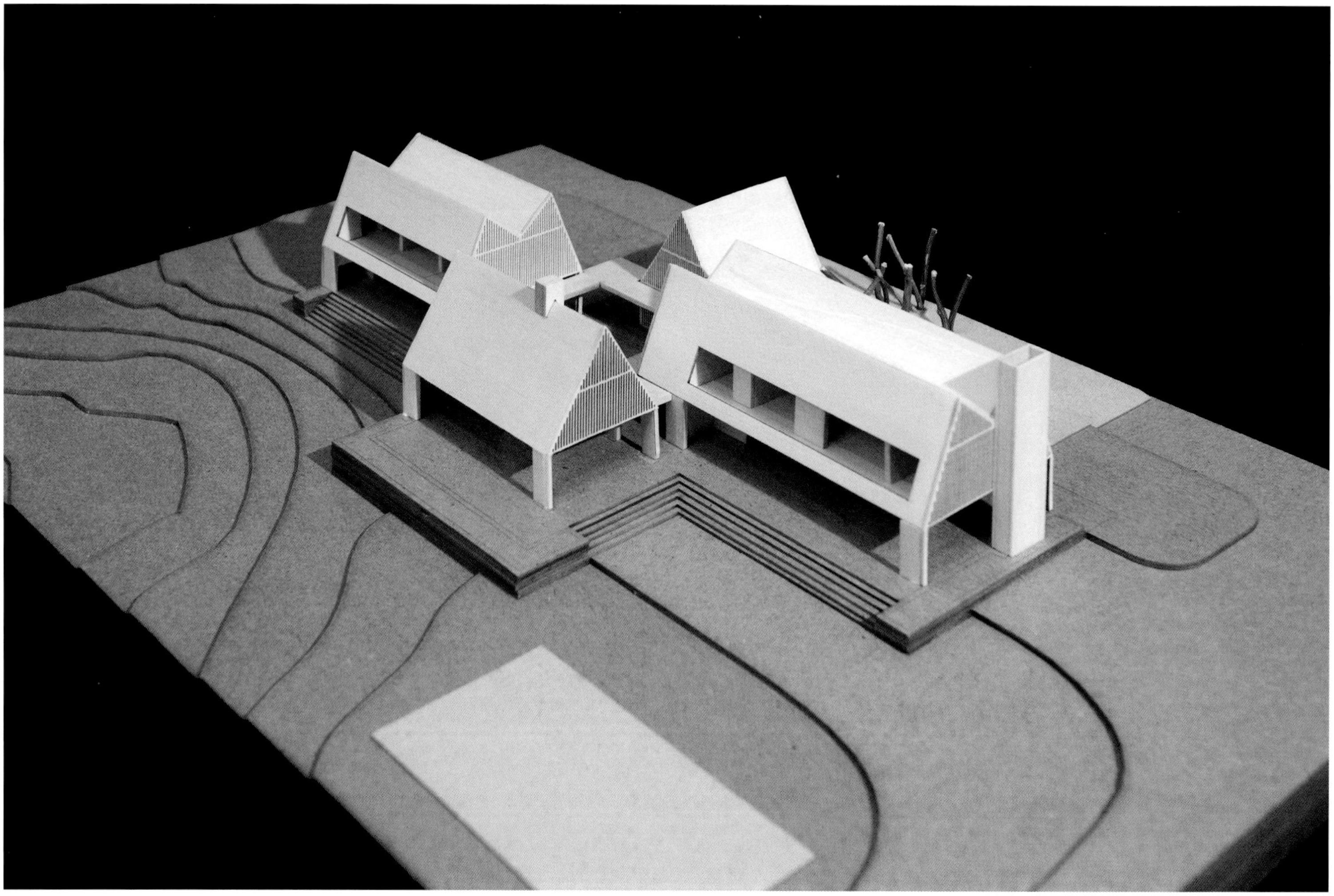

SITE PLAN

1. Parking
2. Entry
3. House
4. Pool
5. Terrace
6. Courtyard
7. Lawn
8. Pond

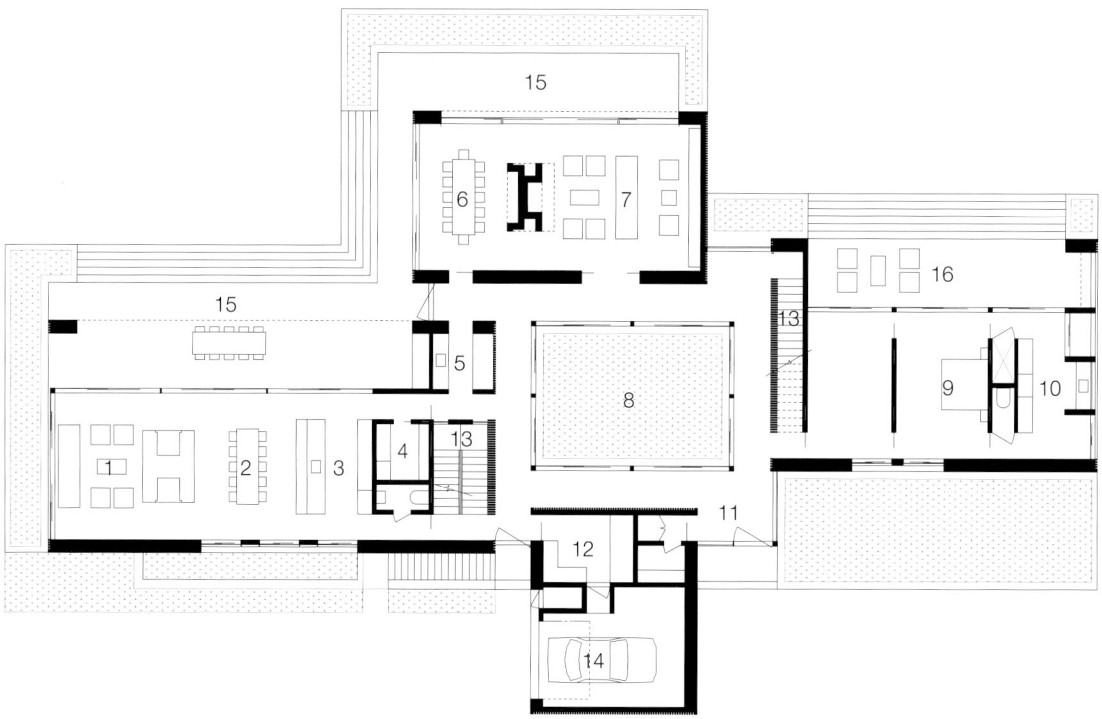

GROUND LEVEL PLAN

1. Family Room
2. Eat-in
3. Kitchen
4. Pantry
5. Bar
6. Dining Room
7. Living Room
8. Courtyard
9. Bedroom
10. Bath
11. Entry
12. Mudroom
13. Stair
14. Garage
15. Terrace

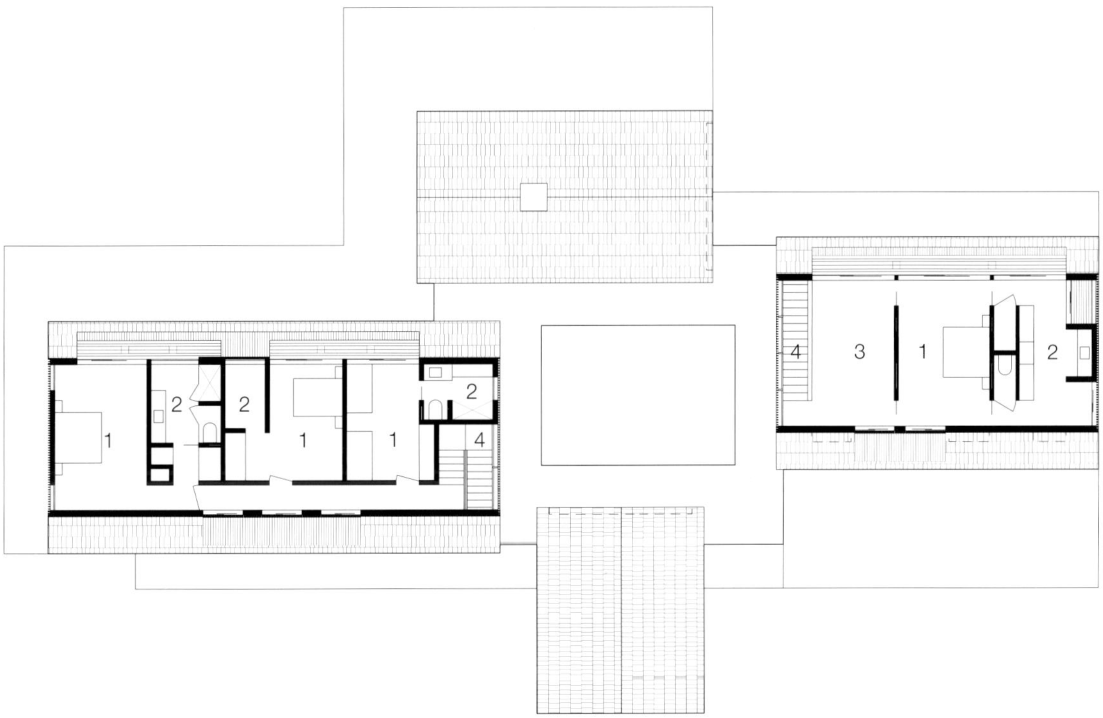

UPPER LEVEL PLAN

1. Bedroom
2. Bath
3. Lounge
4. Stair

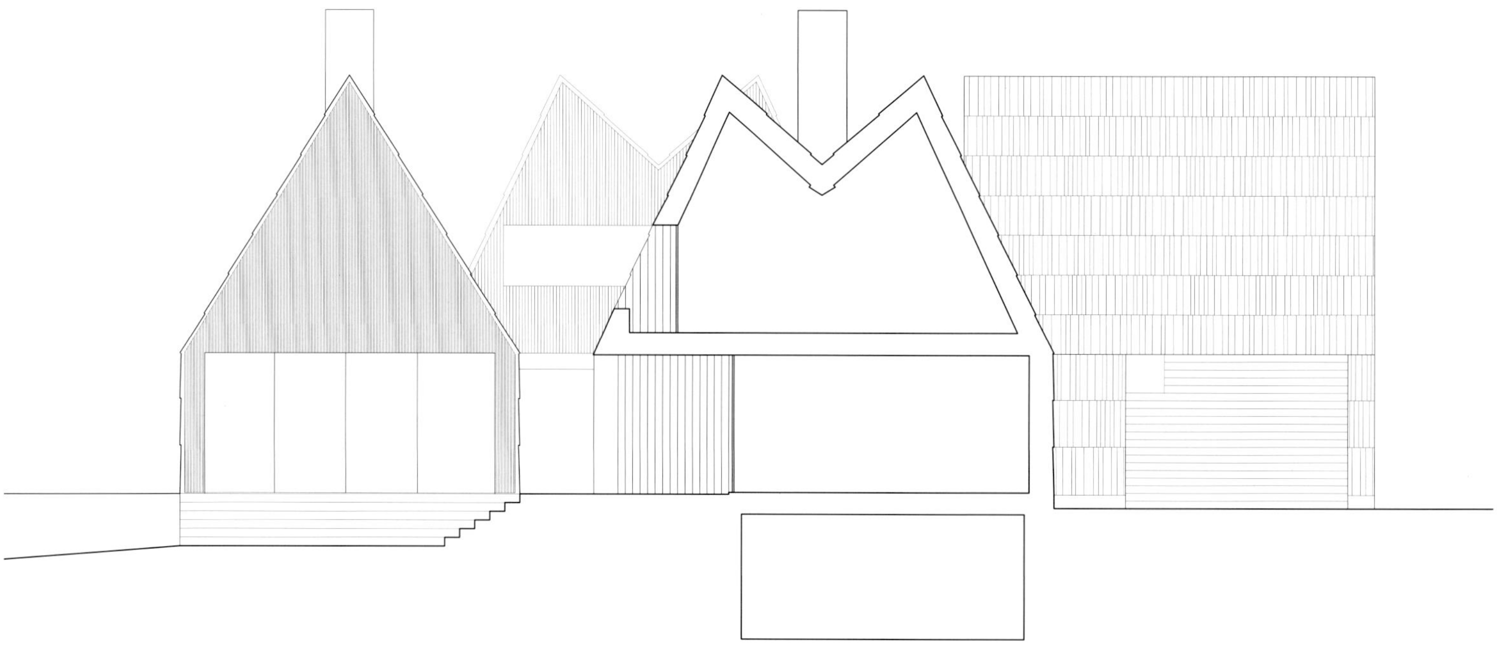

Overlap of multiple structures.

Plinth elevates structure above flood plane.

Assignment of individual functions to independent volumes allows scalability of the home.

UNDERHILL

2017

A couple that relocated to the suburbs as a compromise between their social and professional lives in the city and the upbringing they wanted for their children sought to create a sense of place on a property with close neighbors on all sides. The solution was inspired by the history of the community they chose, which was an early Quaker settlement. Based on the Quaker tenets of simplicity, humility, and inner focus, the house is broken into a series of modest gabled structures, each one focused inward on its own garden courtyard instead of out to the surrounding neighbors.

The simplicity of each courtyard distills the experience of nature, encouraging one to appreciate its subtleties. Every interior space is connected to the exterior on two sides. The layering of spaces from exterior to interior to courtyard collapses the boundaries between them. From selected vantage points, one may see across multiple spaces and courtyards to framed views beyond. Each volume has a sculpted roof that funnels light and air into the center of the structure.

These pitched roof forms, which reference the early Quaker settlement buildings in the area, are used as a motif in the site design as well to intertwine the structures with the landscape. The roof's inverse profile is carved out of the earth to create a lower courtyard at the basement level. Planted retaining walls slope down to let light and air into the lower level.

Similarly, a sunken area with sloped sides forms a destination in the landscape where a grove of trees grows, creating a contemplative spot much like the interior courtyards.

The detailing of interior materials accentuates the central courtyards. The oak floor and weathered oak ceiling boards both radiate outwards from the center. They are custom cut in width and mitered to trace continuously and concentrically around the courtyards. Weathered-metal straps on the ceiling accent this geometry and become armatures for lighting and audiovisual equipment throughout the house.

On the exterior, a limited number of materials are carefully detailed to accentuate the geometric form of each pavilion. A pronounced shadow line traces around each building and articulates the scale of the oversized shingles and undercoursing layer. On the roof, the shingles are an ideal material as they accommodate tapering courses that follow the roof's compound pitches. At areas below grade, bluestone is cut to the same size and shape and applied in a shingled manner on the chimney to retain the uniformity of the volumes.

The Quaker values of simplicity and craft tie the new home to the community. Using the courtyard as a device to bring light and nature into the interior of each volume results in an inward-looking and contemplative home that establishes the sense of place the parents sought for their family.

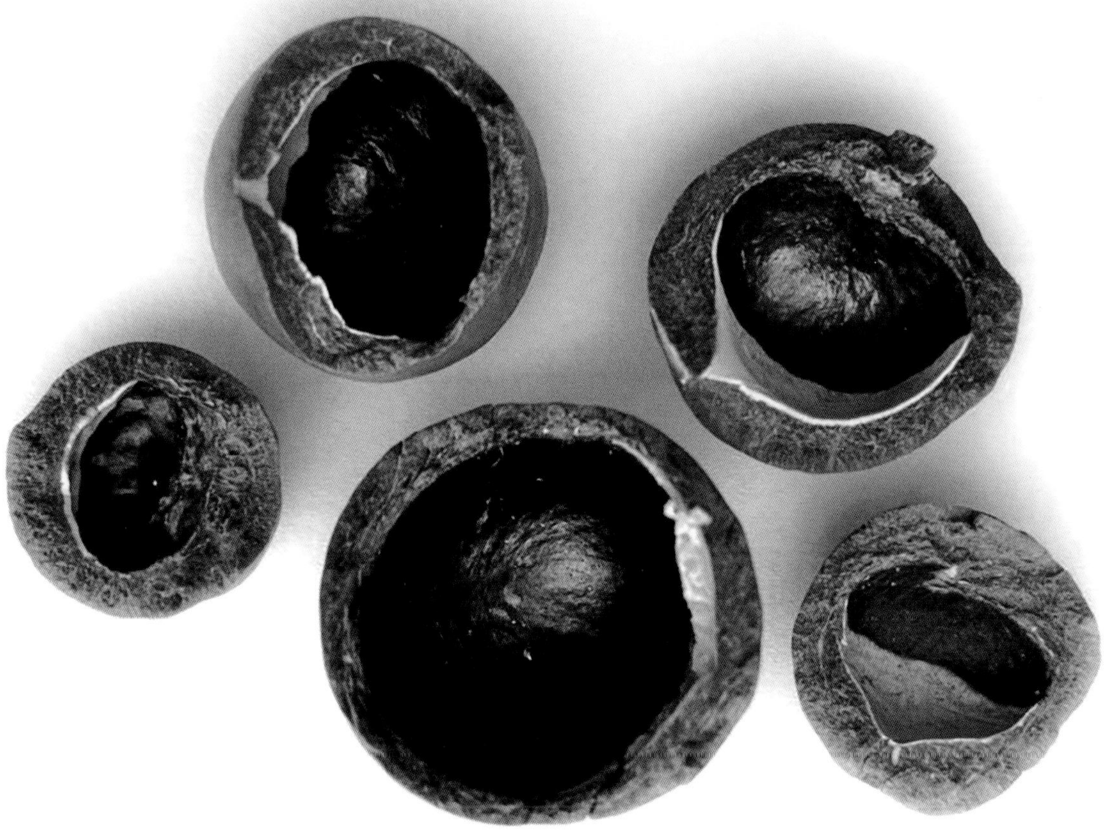

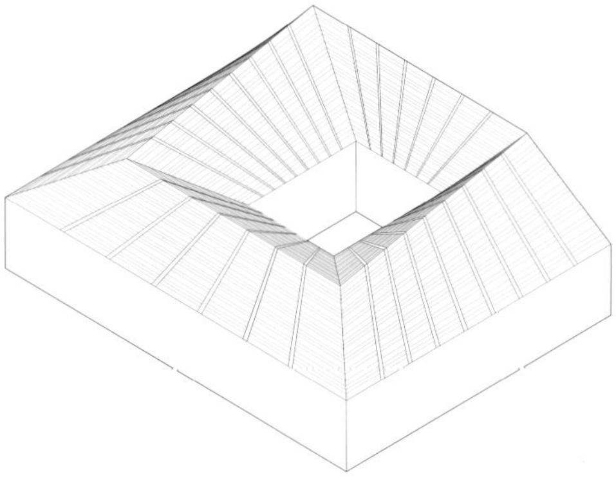

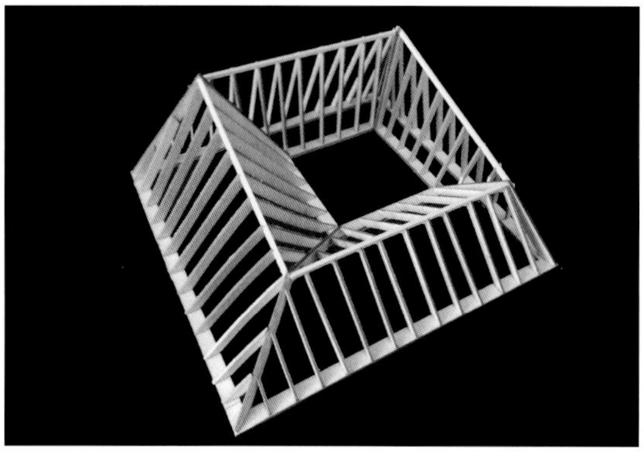

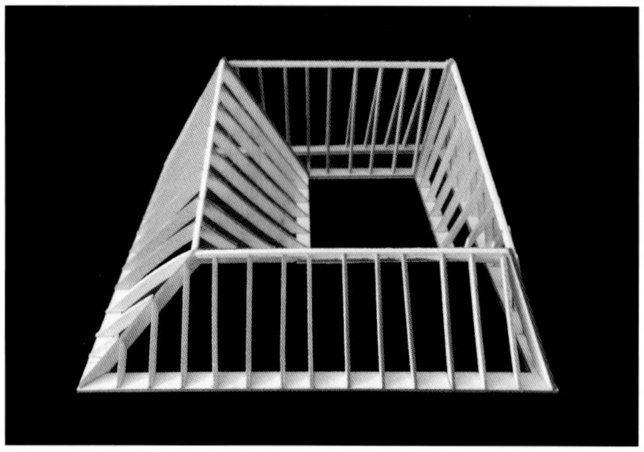

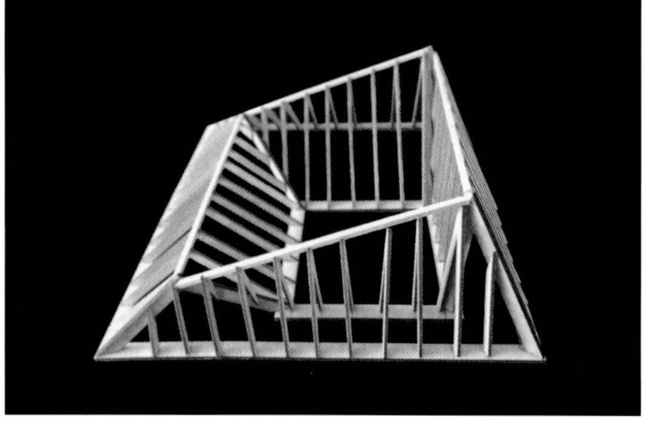

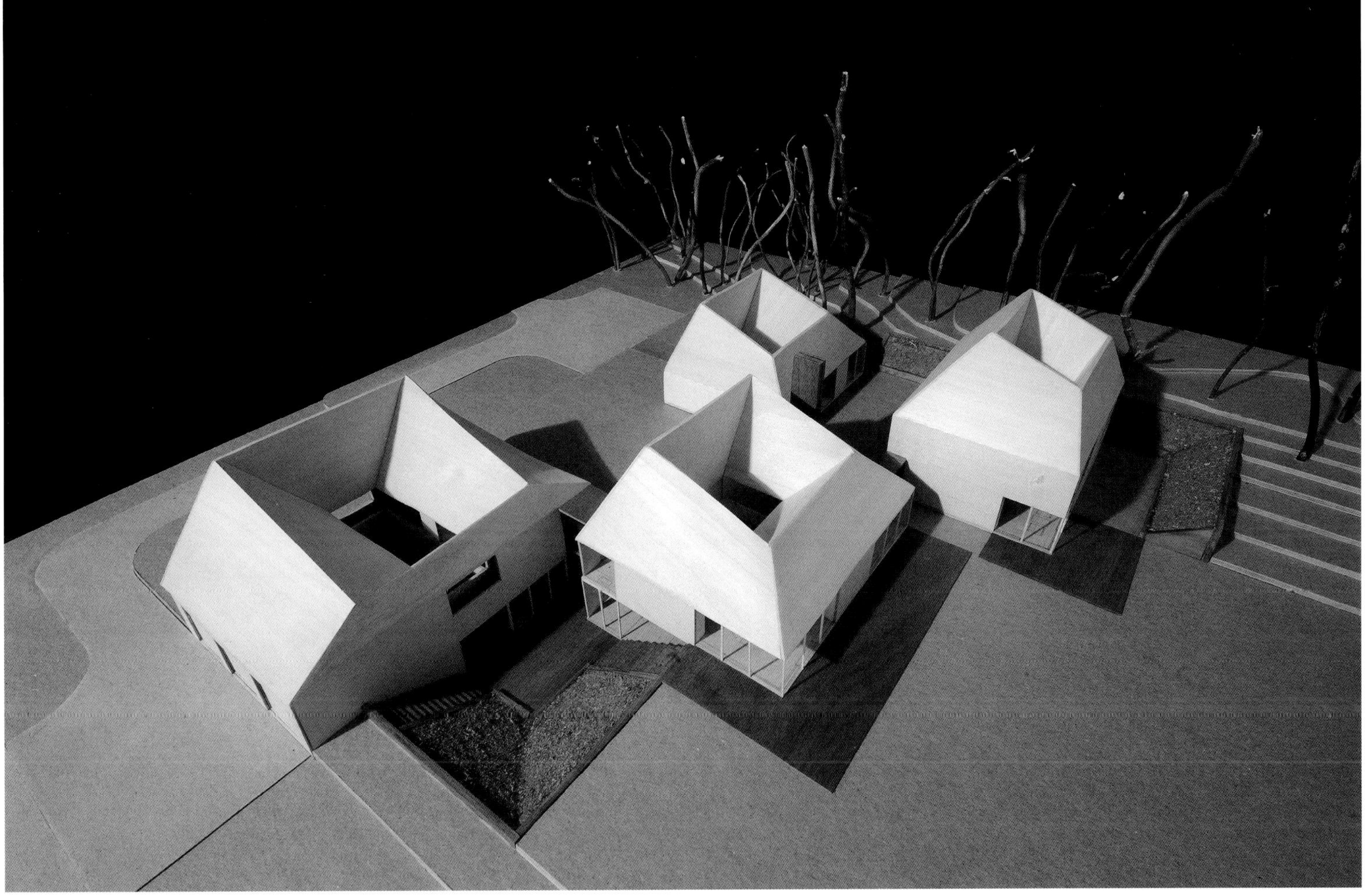

SITE PLAN

1. House
2. Shed
3. Driveway
4. Parking
5. Lawn
6. Terrace
7. Courtyard

SECTION

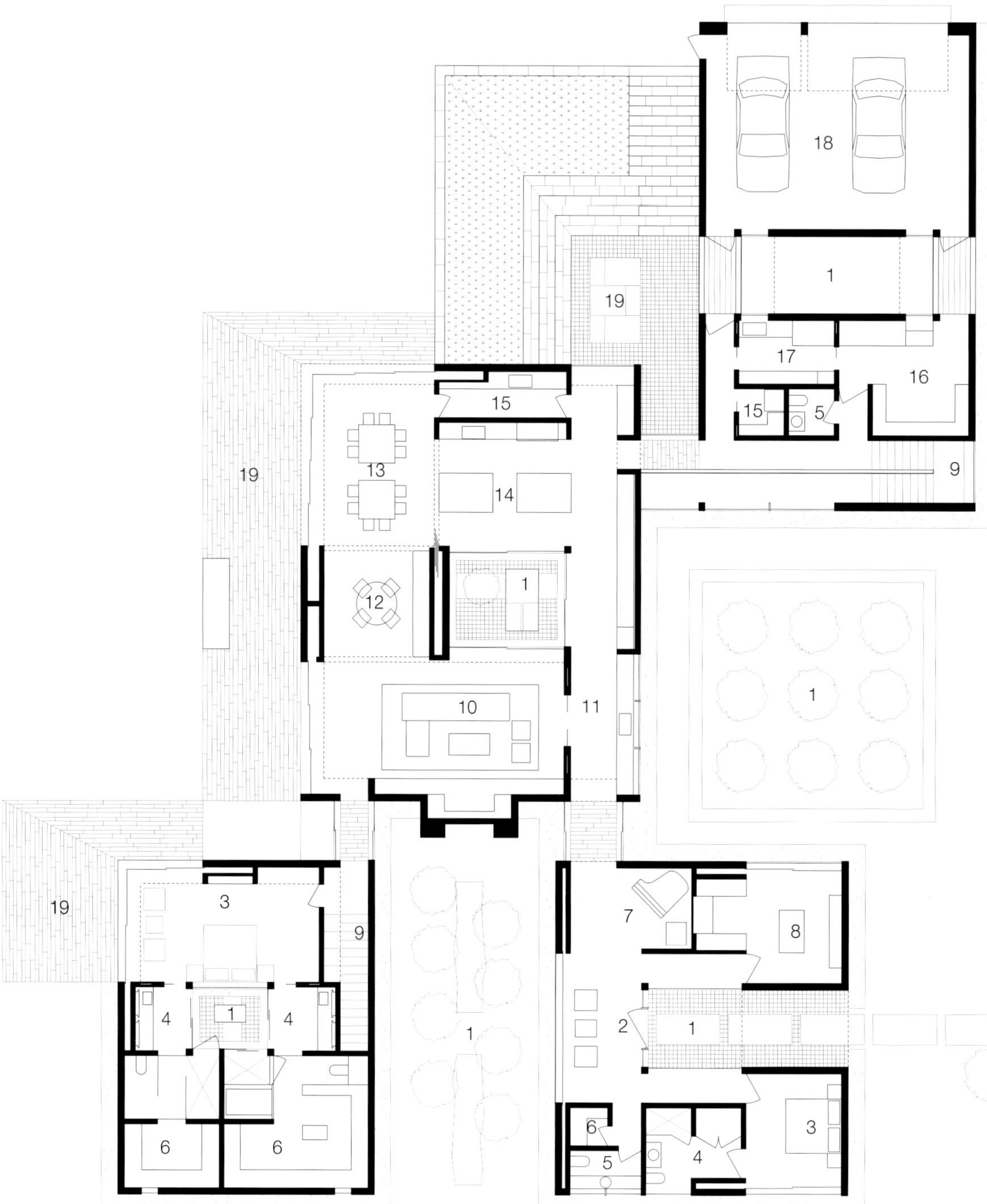

GROUND LEVEL PLAN

1. Courtyard
2. Entry
3. Bedroom
4. Bath
5. Powder Room
6. Closet
7. Sitting Room
8. Office
9. Stair
10. Family Room
11. Bar
12. Shared Room
13. Dining Room
14. Kitchen
15. Pantry
16. Mudroom
17. Laundry
18. Garage
19. Terrace

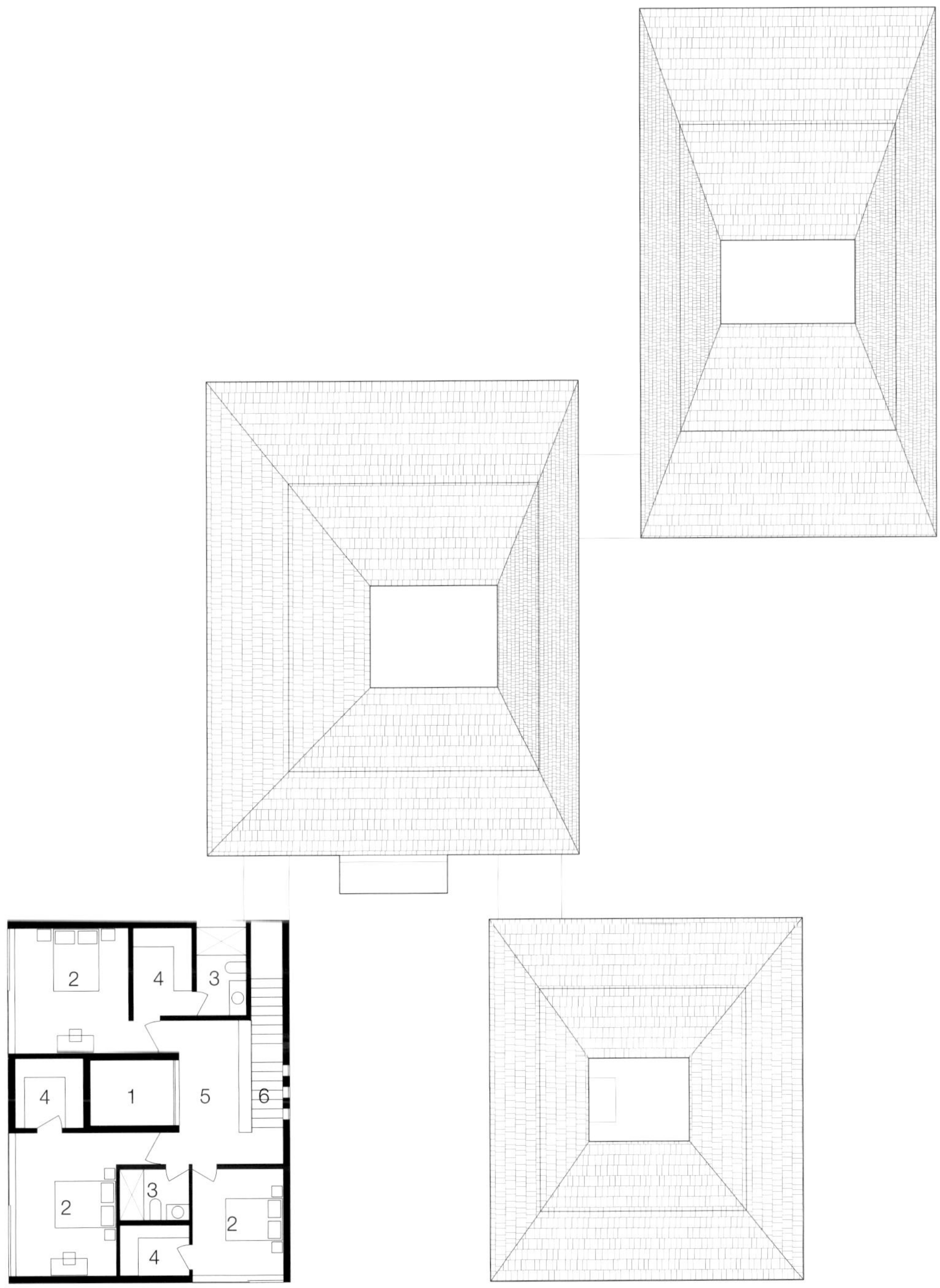

UPPER LEVEL PLAN

1. Courtyard
2. Bedroom
3. Bath
4. Closet
5. Hall
6. Stair

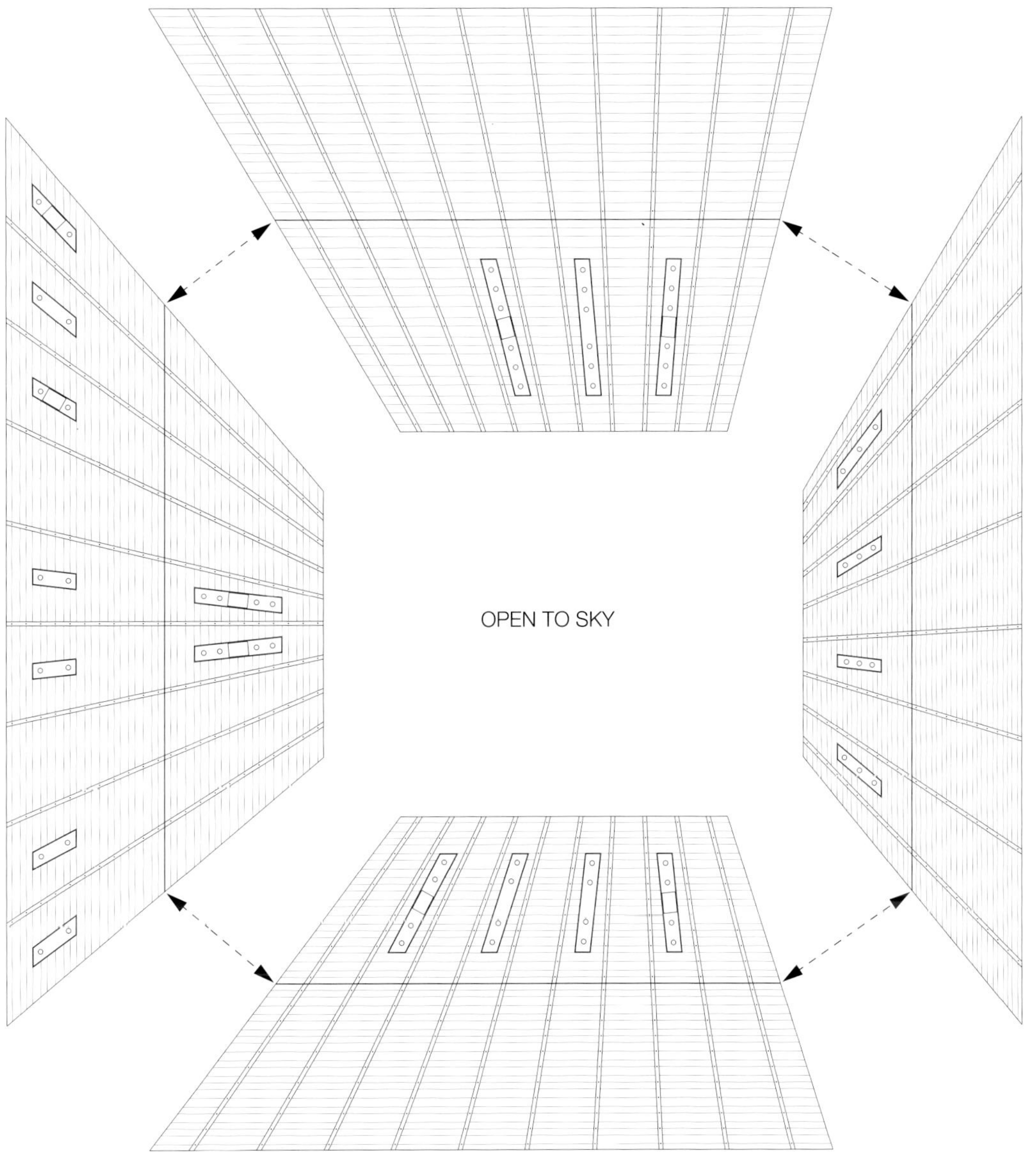

Radiating ceiling reinforces inward focus.

Exterior connection to entry.

Interior connection between structures.

WOLF

Roof's inverse form carved into the landscape.

ACTON COVE

2017

An active family with a love of boating wanted a home on Chesapeake Bay, surrounded by the maritime charm of Annapolis Harbor. They found a small but spectacular lot with a house on it from the 1970s. The existing house did not meet the owners' needs but its bulkheads and docks provided a unique opportunity: the chance to build a home just steps from the water in downtown Annapolis. As the previous house was demolished, layer upon layer of old bulkheads and fill revealed how generations of previous owners had expanded the site into the harbor and reinforced it from the elements. This process of layering inspired the solution to the current design challenges–the harsh coastal environment and the privacy issues of being in close proximity to neighbors and active waterways. The new design configures layers of site features and envelope elements to provide privacy and weather protection, while encouraging connections to the outdoors.

The outermost layer is the bulkhead itself, on top of which sits a boardwalk of 2x8 ipe decking that connects several docks on the property. Stepped weathering steel planters mediate between the boardwalk level and the ground level, which is elevated above the flood plane. Deep overhangs protect the house and provide shade to the decks that surround it. The second floor, also encircled by cantilevered decks and balconies, is wrapped in layers of fixed ipe screens and operable canvas drapes. Riding in a continuous track along the entire perimeter, the drapes can be configured to provide privacy at the master balcony, a wind block at the outdoor fireplace, or shade for the outdoor dining area. The large expanses of glass are also operable, pocketing into the adjacent walls to merge the indoor and outdoor spaces completely, or providing the option of insect screens. Interior linen drapes and roll shades provide the last layer of operable screening. The multiple layers can be configured for a variety of activities requiring different levels of privacy, and for different weather conditions, extending the time the family spends outdoors.

The materials of the various layers reflect the character of the working harbor. Weathering steel planters reference sheet pilings. 3x14 reclaimed heart pine siding is reminiscent of heavy timber bulkheads. Oversize silicone bronze screws, left exposed to fasten the siding, are pulled from the ship building industry. Woven rope and sailcloth details draw on local crafts. These traditional materials, layered with modern insulation, glazing, and building systems, create a high-performance structure, contributing to the LEED Certification of the house.

In its thoughtful layering of envelope and site elements, the design connects the house and its owners with the best aspects of the environment, while providing shelter from the challenging elements.

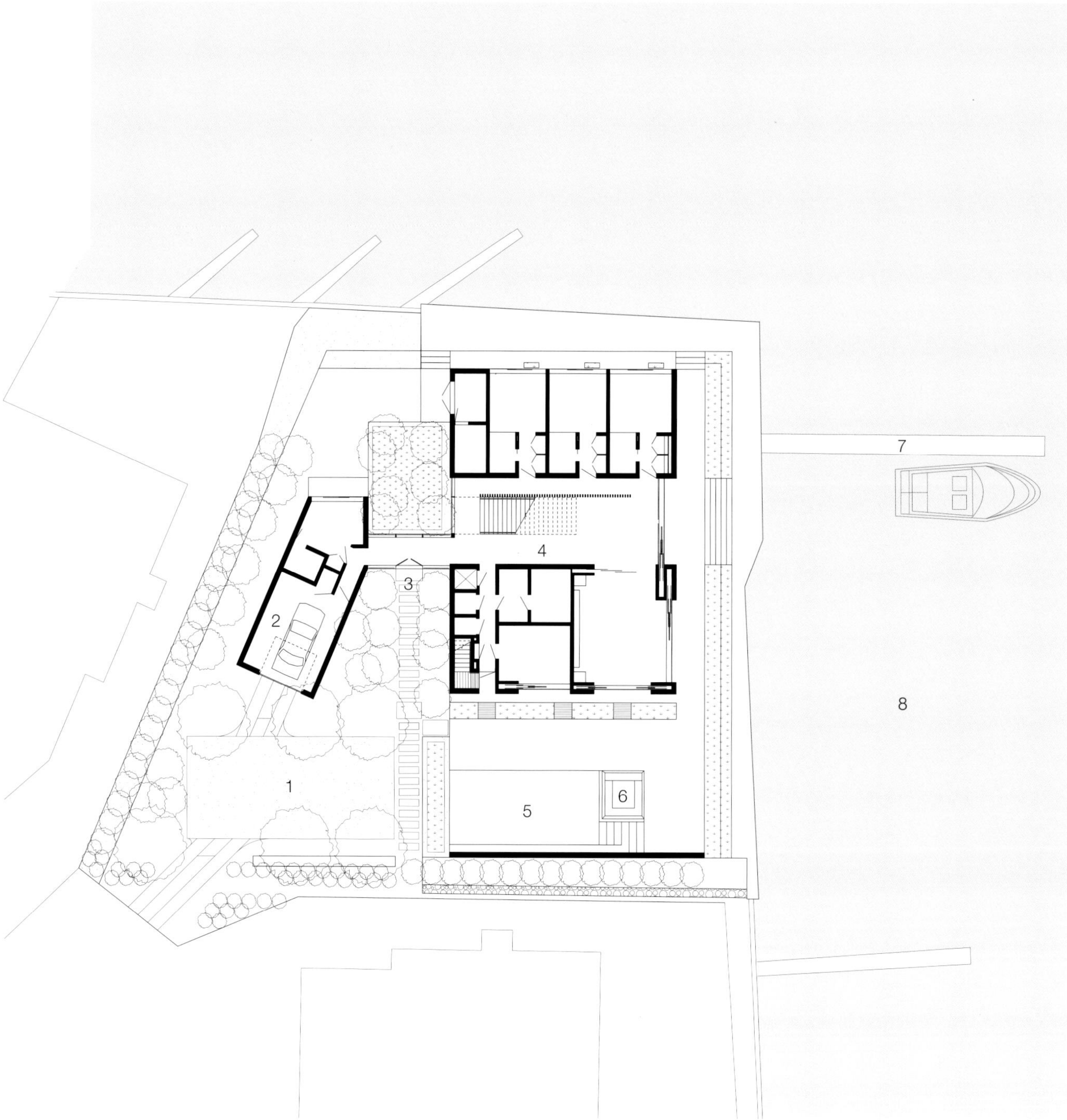

SITE PLAN

1. Parking
2. Garage
3. Entry
4. House
5. Pool
6. Spa
7. Dock
8. Cove

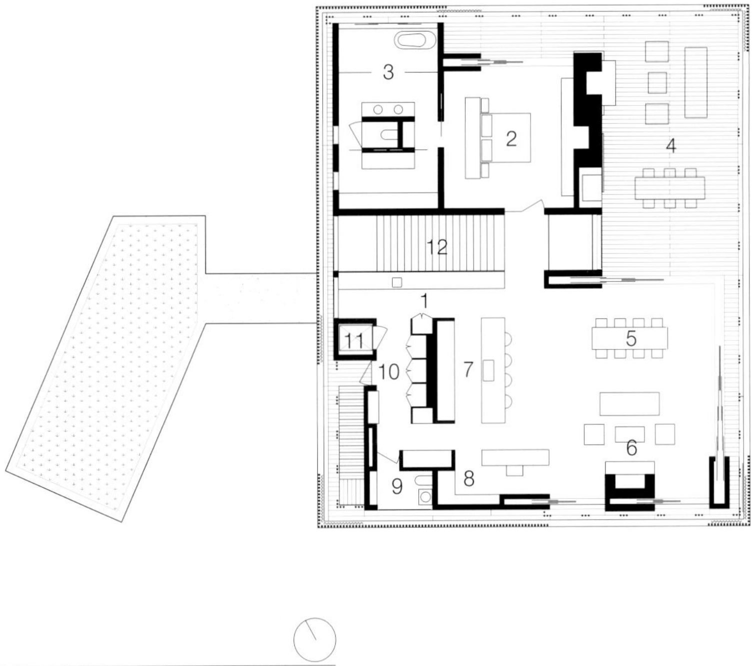

UPPER LEVEL PLAN

1. Wet Bar
2. Bedroom
3. Bath
4. Deck
5. Dining
6. Living
7. Kitchen
8. Office
9. Powder Room
10. Pantry
11. Elevator
12. Stair

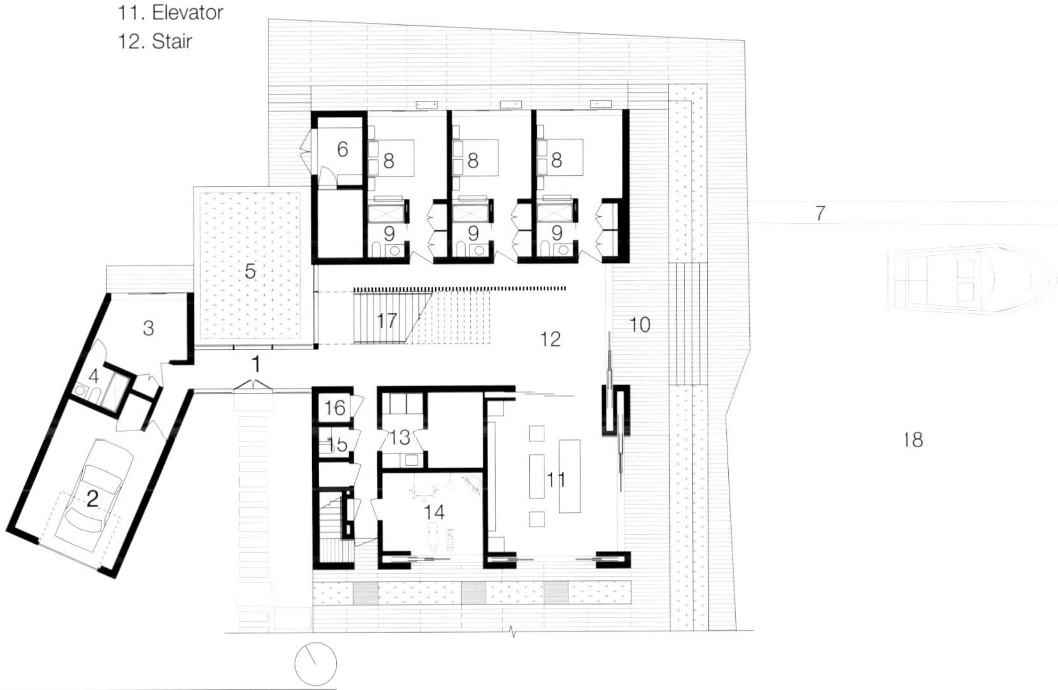

GROUND LEVEL PLAN

1. Entry
2. Garage
3. Studio
4. Studio Bath
5. Garden
6. Boat Storage
7. Dock
8. Bedroom
9. Bath
10. Deck
11. Family Room
12. Multi-Purpose
13. Laundry
14. Gym
15. Powder Room
16. Elevator
17. Stair
18. Acton Cove

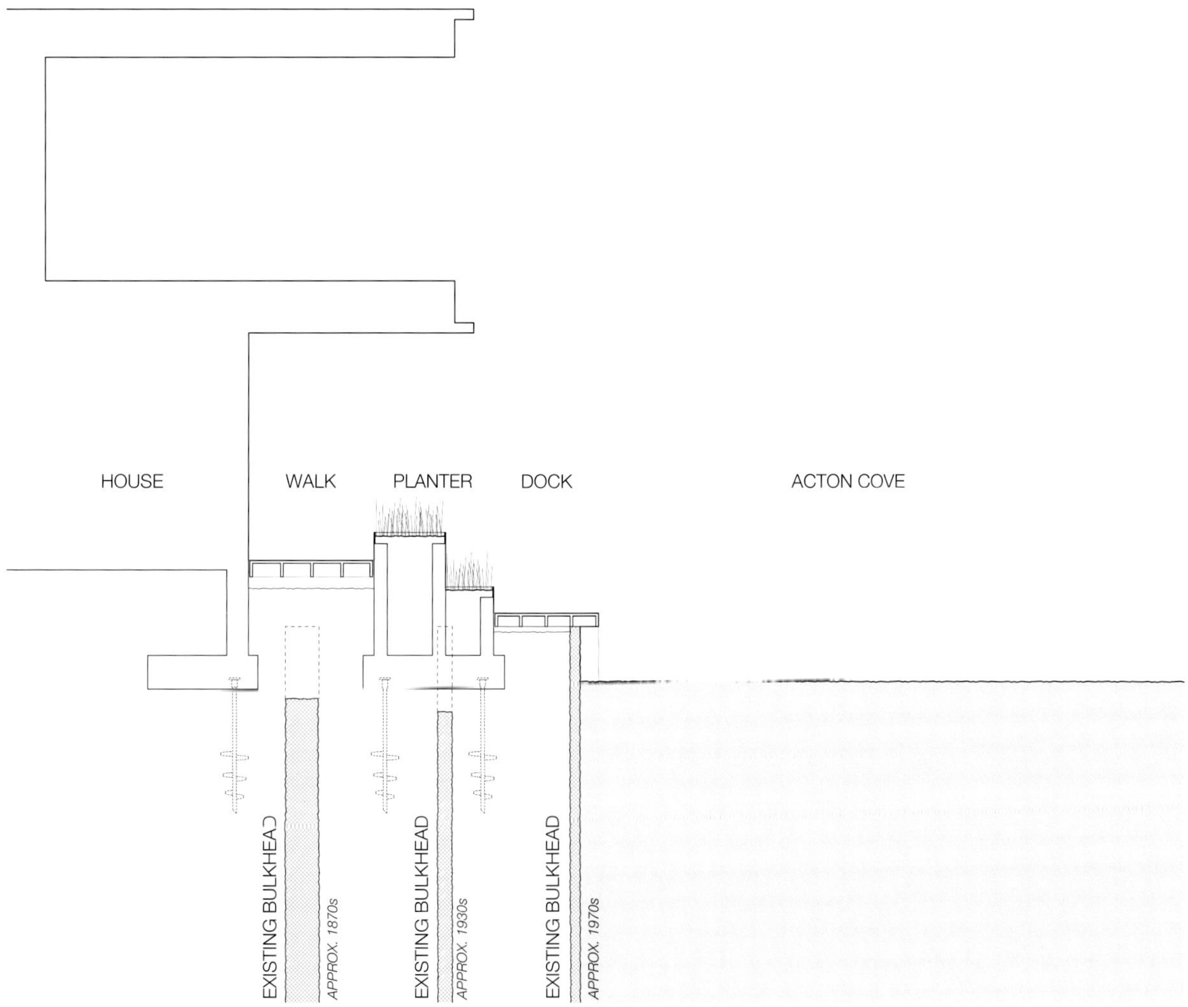

New construction on helical piles parallels layers of historic bulkhead structures.

BLACK SHEEP

Opposite: Layers of screen, exterior drapery, operable glazing, interior drapery.

Layering of indoor and outdoor spaces.

SAGG FARM

2018

Sagaponack, with its flat terrain and fertile loam, has historically been a farming community set within the resort enclaves on the East End of Long Island. The open expanses of its potato fields sat in contrast to the forests and gardens of the surroundings. In recent years, fueled by its proximity to the ocean, the tide of development in Sagaponack has been steady and inevitable. Farm fields have given way to residential subdivisions. This project seeks to honor the agricultural traditions of the area by applying the fundamental principles of agriculture to architecture: placing order on nature and maximizing access to light and air.

The majority of crops in Sagaponack were row crops as opposed to field crops, they were spaced apart in ordered lines to maximize each plants' exposure to sunlight. In this region, rows were oriented north/south so as not to shade one another and to align with the prevailing southerly wind, thereby improving pollination and reducing erosion. Acres of north/south rows gave the community a grain and orientation. These principles are applied to the form of the house, which is separated into parallel bars spaced equidistant apart to admit sunlight and fresh air. Breezeways of operable glazing connect the more solid bar forms while allowing the passage of light and wind. The plantings, trees, and paving of the landscape design, which are similarly organized into parallel rows, extend between the bars of the house into the courtyards, intertwining the house and the land. Breaking the home into multiple volumes has the added benefits of reducing its apparent mass and enhancing the privacy between spaces.

Agriculture juxtaposes organic plant forms with meticulously cultivated straight rows. This beautiful contrast inspired the treatment of materials in the architecture. The dimensions of the house are broken down to a 4' module in both plan and section. This three-dimensional grid governs the placement of everything from walls to light fixtures. Materials are selected and manipulated to defy the strict order. The rainscreen siding of thin cedar strips was installed green and fastened with only two screws at the center. The unfastened ends of each board are free to warp according to their grain direction, creating an organic pattern within the rigid framework. The pattern will further change over time depending on the exposure to the sun and rain. Inside, stone with prominent veining was selected to contrast the otherwise crisp lines. At the stair, rows of wood balusters are free to rotate around their supports. Felt louvers on each baluster serve as acoustic absorbers and catch the wind or a passing hand to rotate the balusters, continually changing the pattern.

What is good for crops is also good for people. And so, by applying the principles of farming to architecture, the house is made more comfortable and more beautiful. At the same time, the disappearing historic character of the place is honored in the design.

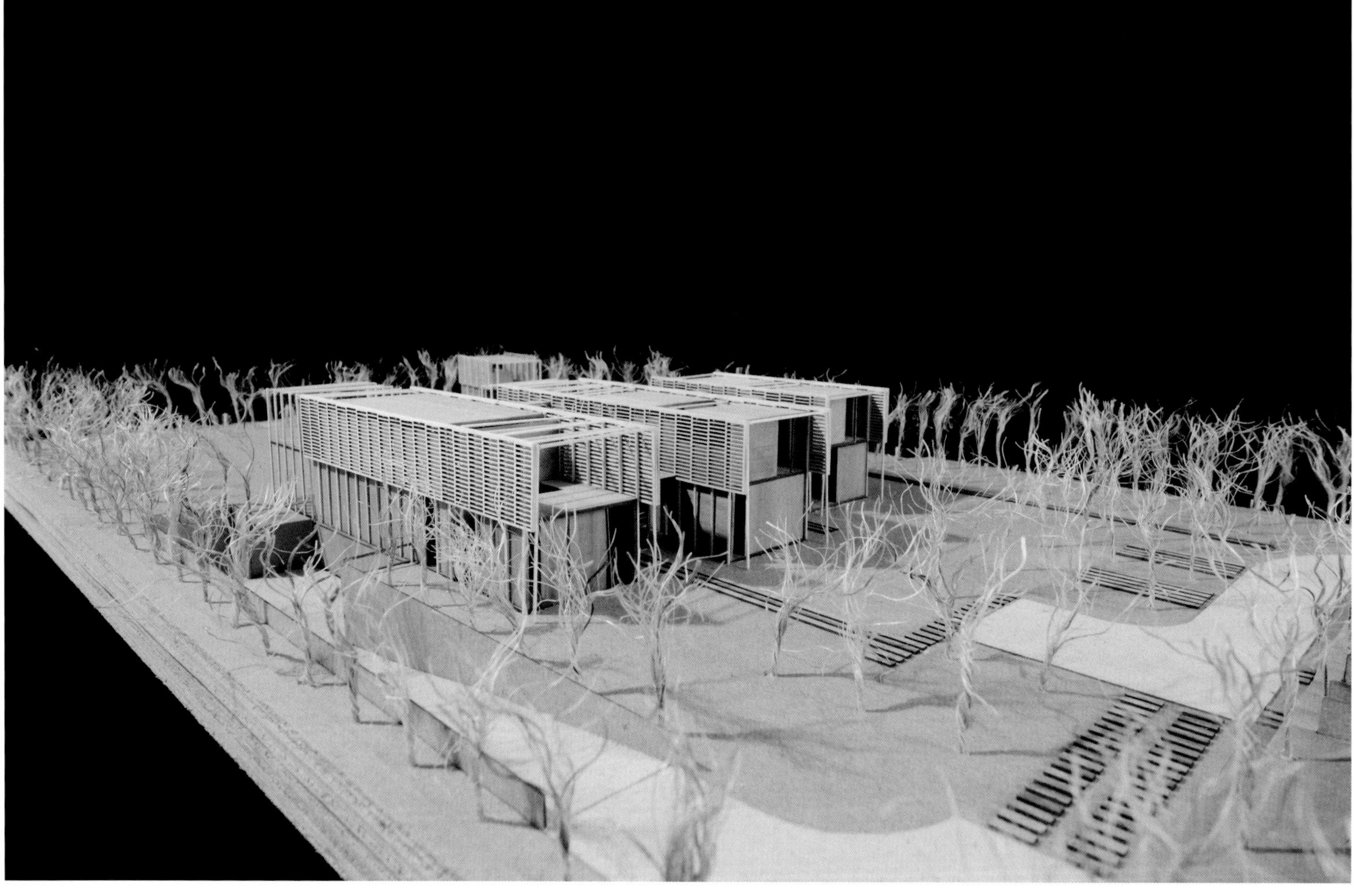

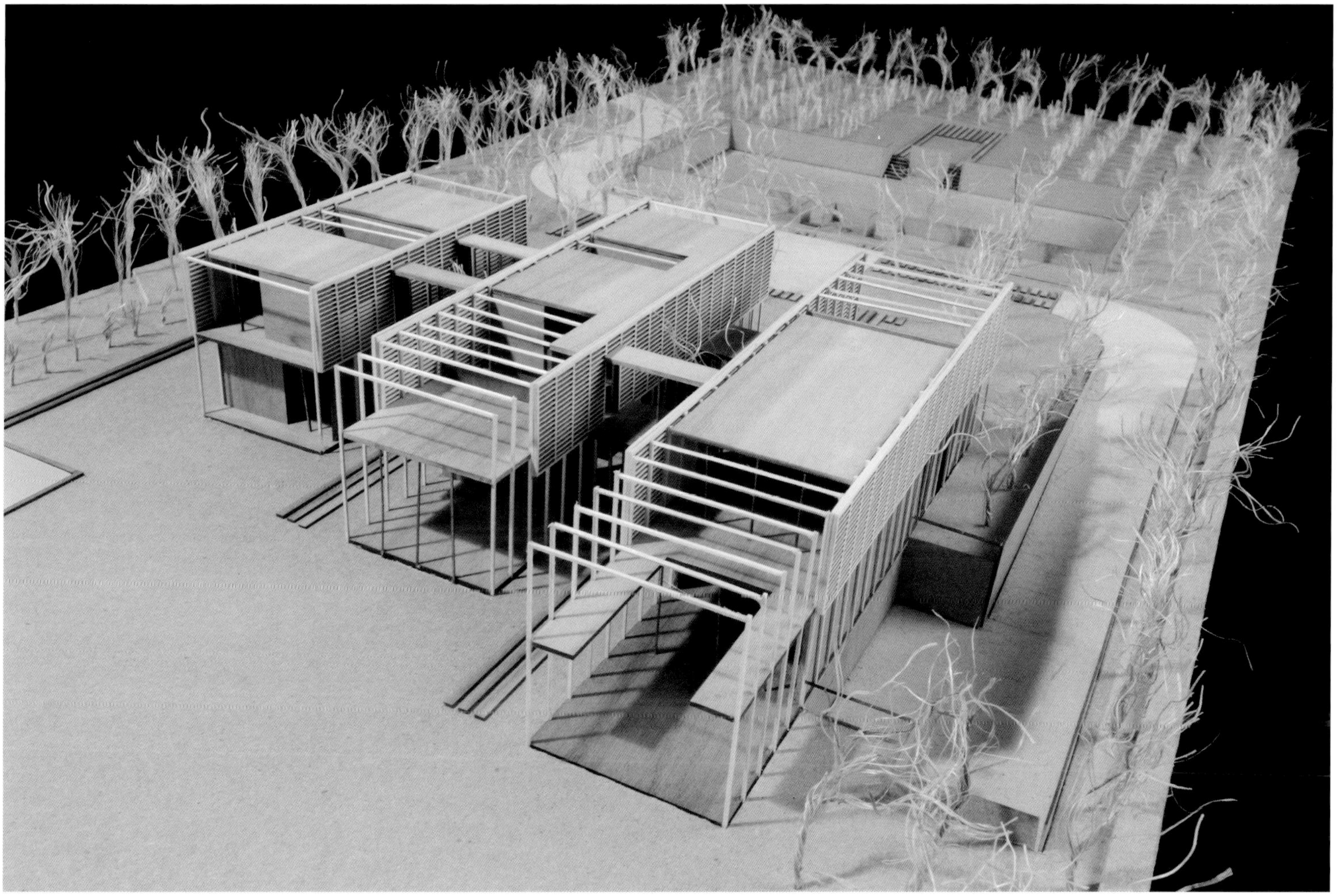

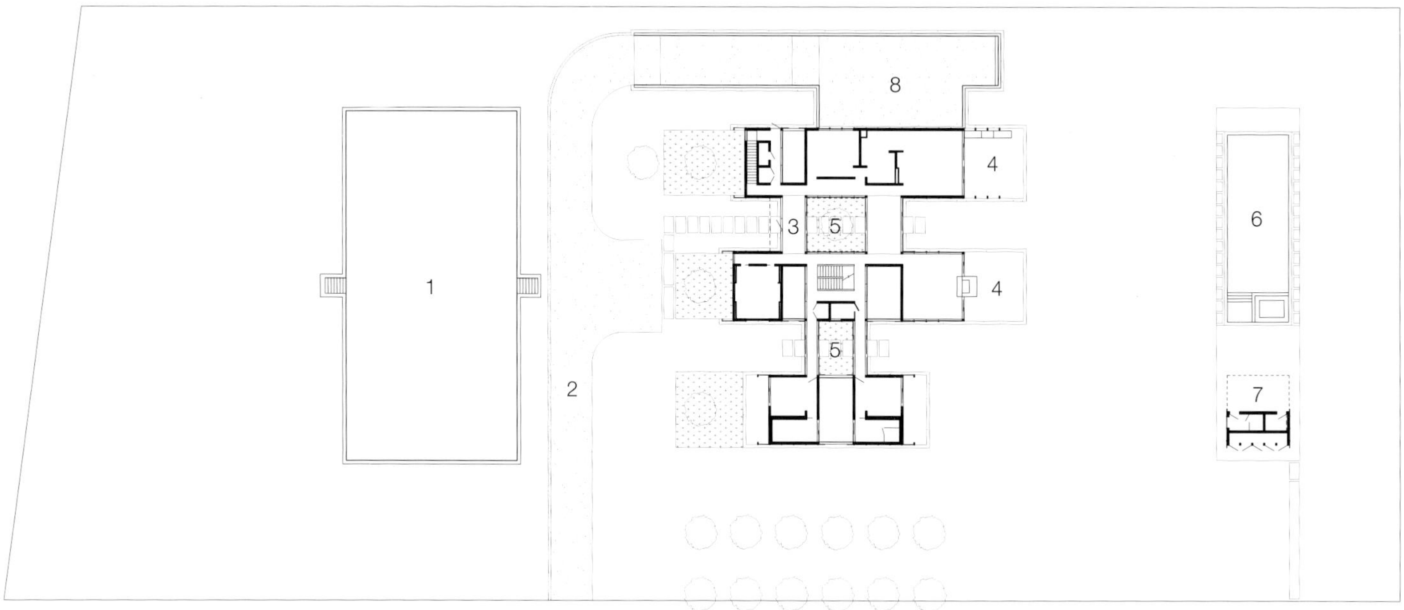

SITE PLAN

1. Tennis Court
2. Driveway
3. Main House
4. Patio
5. Courtyard
6. Pool
7. Pool House
8. Parking

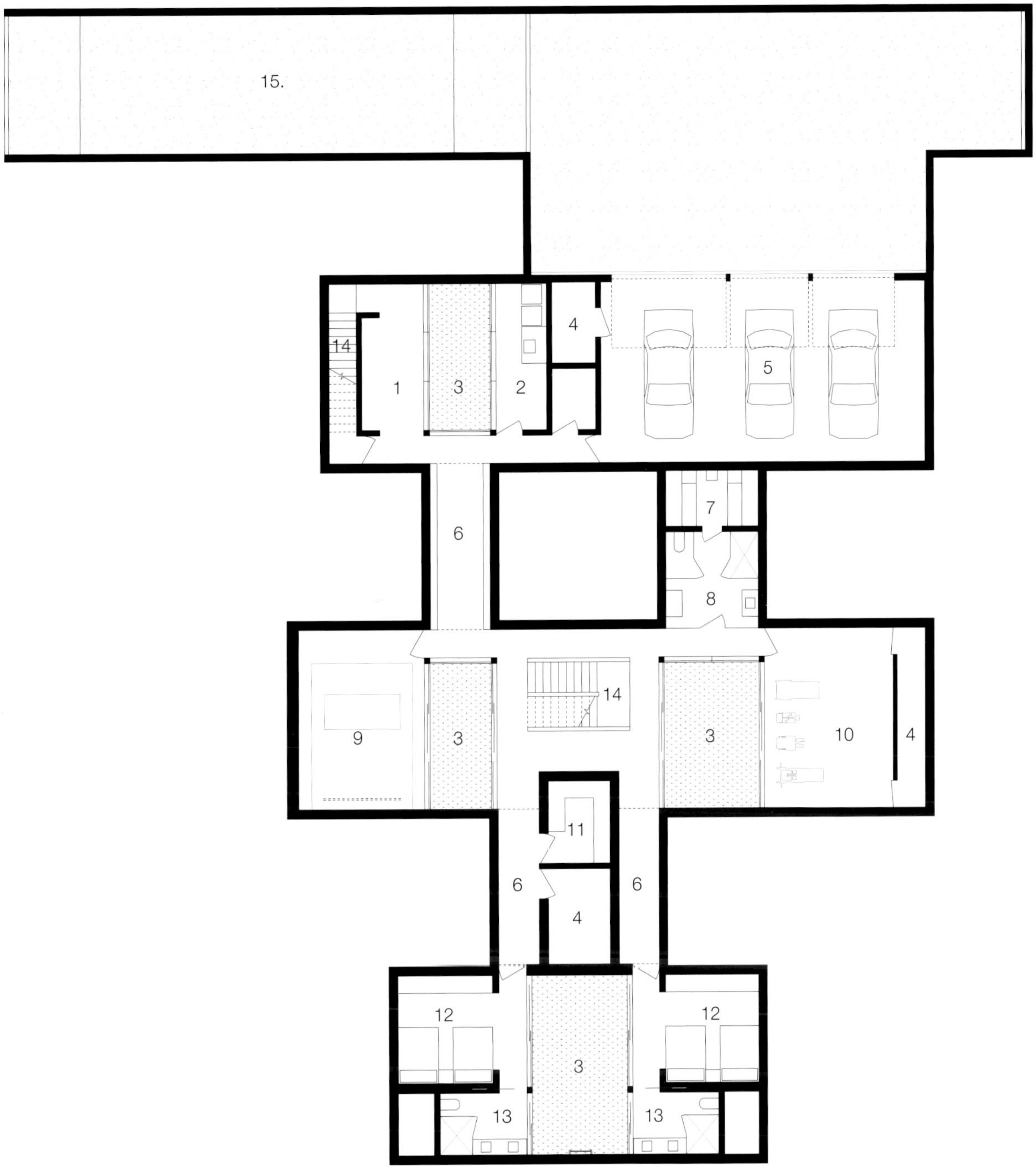

LOWER LEVEL PLAN

1. Mud Room
2. Laundry
3. Courtyard
4. Mechanical
5. Garage
6. Hall
7. Sauna
8. Gym Bath
9. Golf Simulator
10. Gym
11. Storage
12. Bedroom
13. Bath
14. Stair
15. Ramp

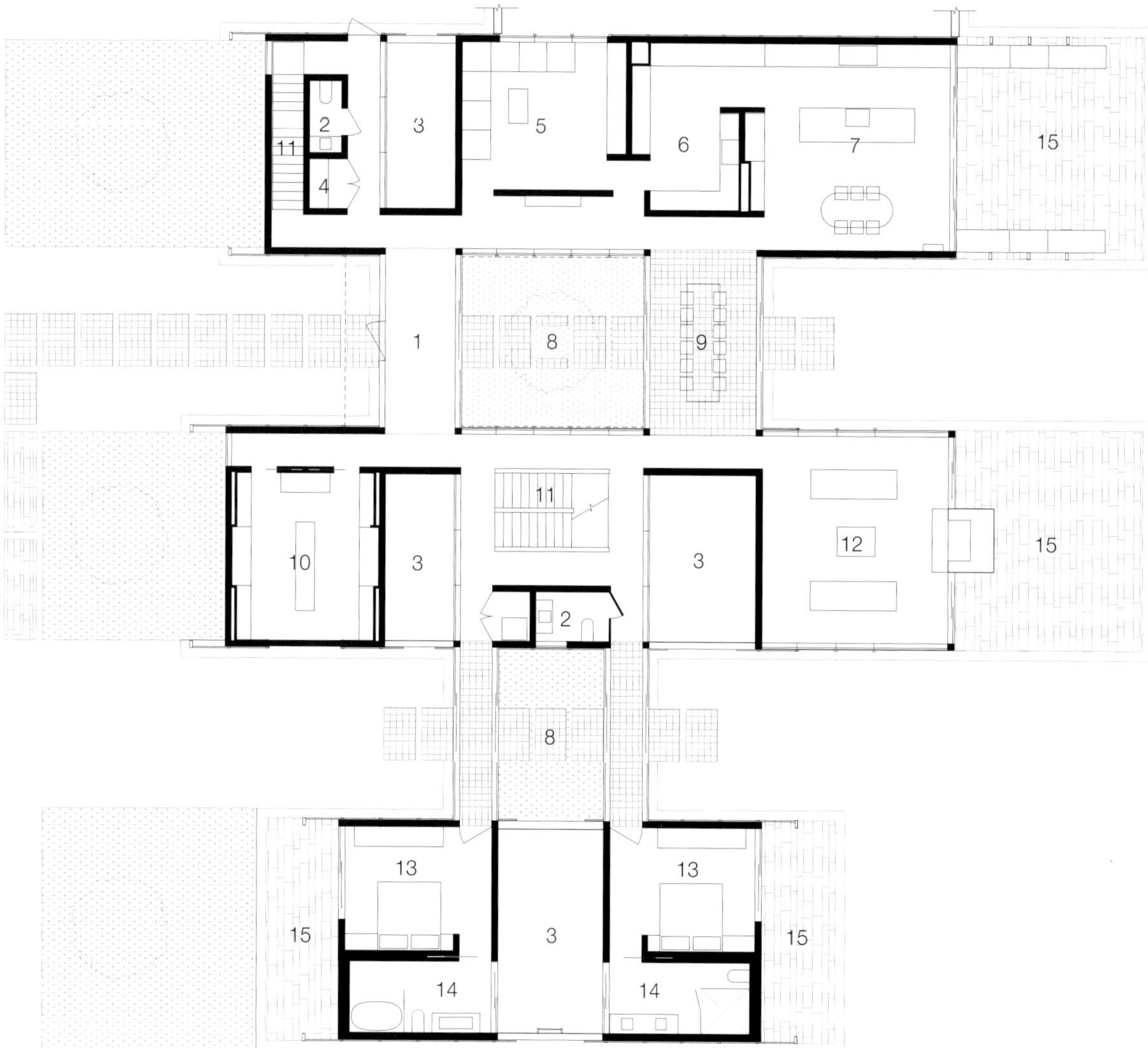

GROUND LEVEL PLAN

1. Entry
2. Powder Room
3. Courtyard Below
4. Coat Closet
5. Den
6. Pantry
7. Kitchen
8. Courtyard
9. Formal Dining
10. Office
11. Stair
12. Living Room
13. Bedroom
14. Bath
15. Patio

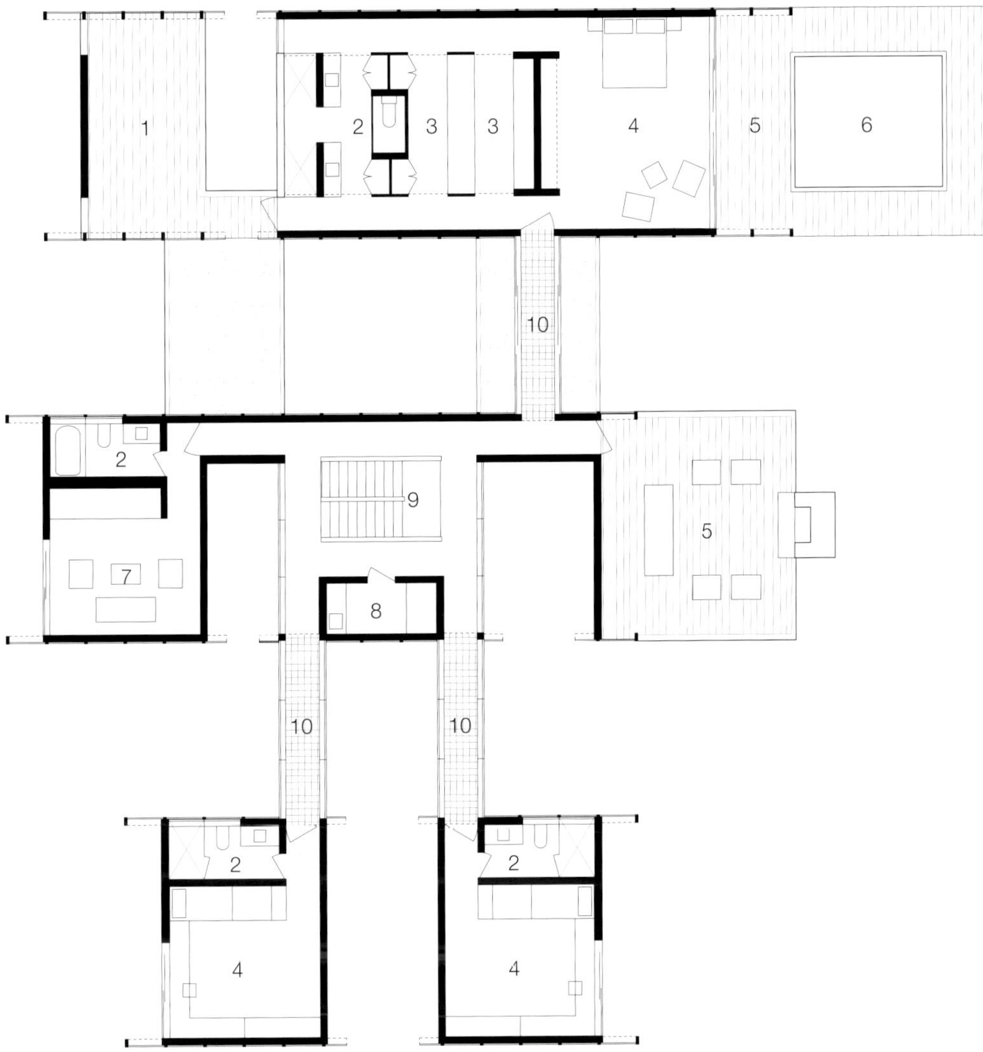

UPPER LEVEL PLAN

1. Outdoor Shower
2. Bath
3. Closet
4. Bedroom
5. Deck
6. Open to Below
7. Playroom
8. Laundry
9. Stair
10. Glass Hall

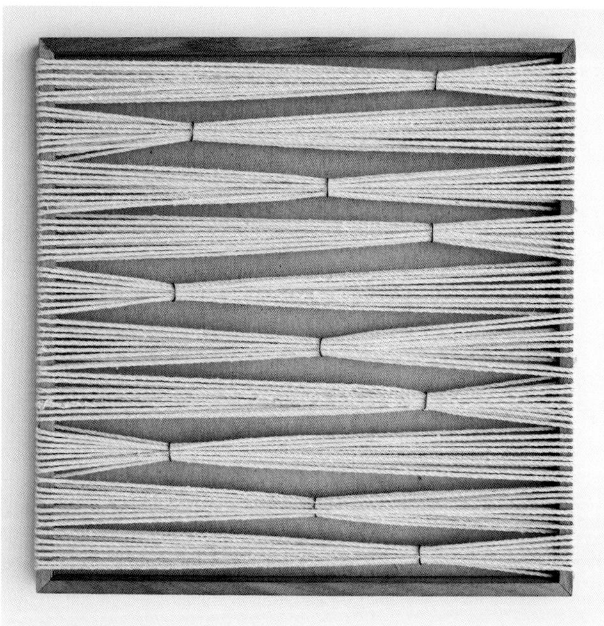

Grouping studies

TimberStrand® LSL

2416

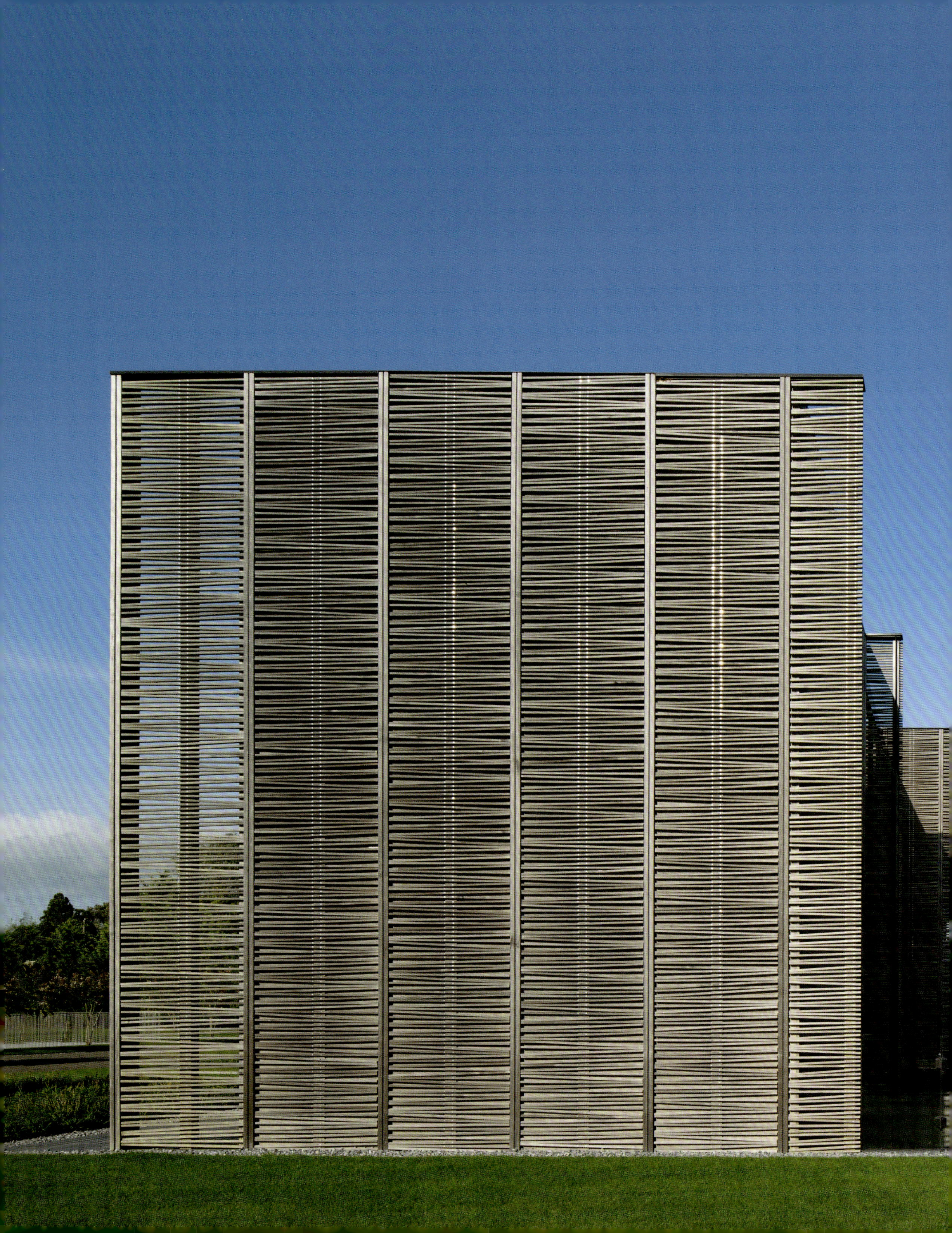

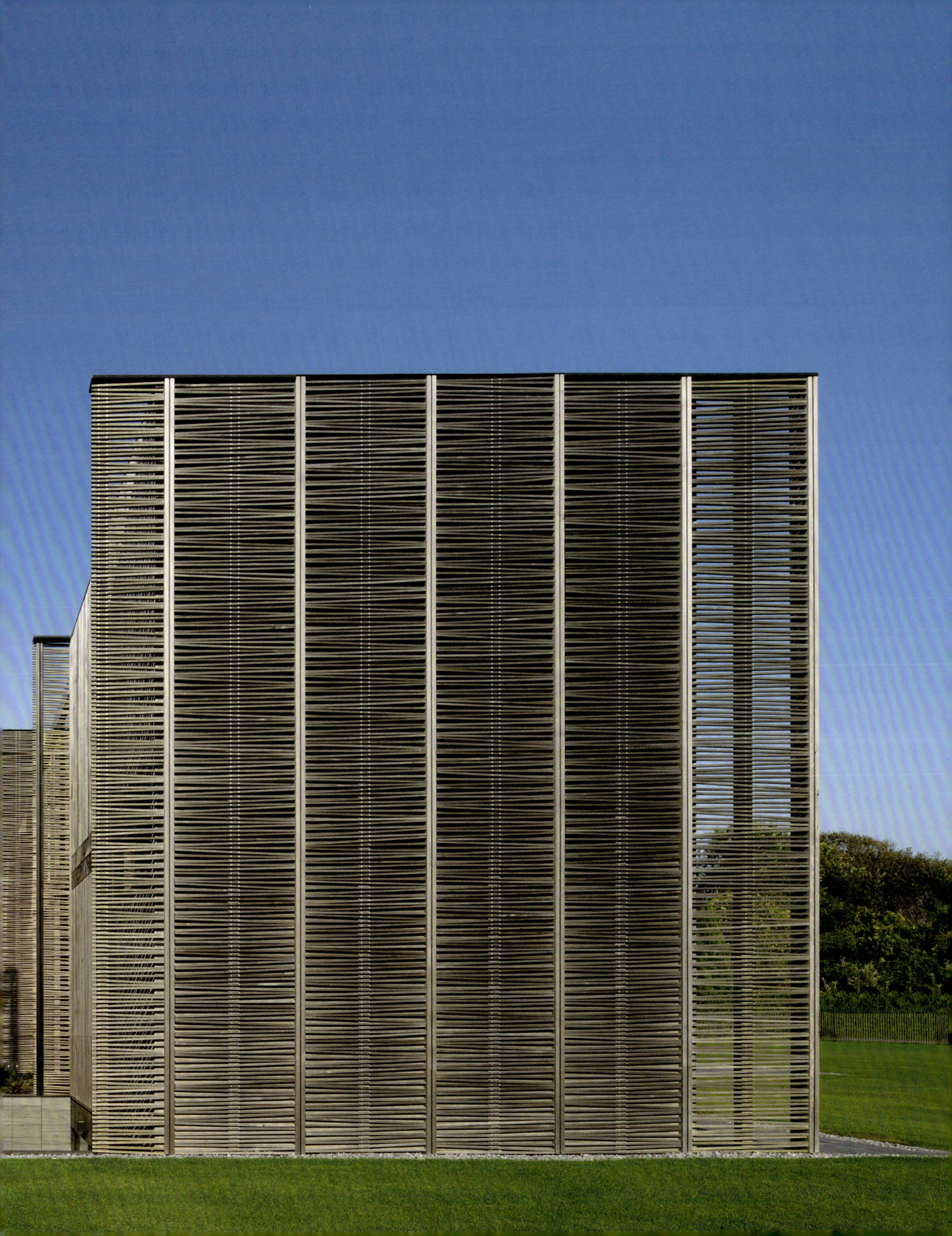

Opposite: Fine breakdown of module with adjustable acoustic louvers.

Reflection of ordered building module within lighting details and material treatments.

K I H T ' H A N

2018

Too often the architectural response to flood-prone sites is to distort conventional designs and methods to meet the flood protection requirements, masking the issue at best. In contrast, the design for this property overlooking a coastal pond and the ocean beyond celebrates the periodically rising water levels. Rather than hiding the flood damage prevention measures, the design takes advantage of them, thereby embracing the duality of the wetland landscape to intertwine nature and built form.

The house, pool, decks, and sanitary field are elevated and broken apart to let flood waters flow around and between them, reducing the potentially damaging hydrodynamic pressure of coastal flooding. Thus, the house becomes a series of vertical volumes from which to observe the ocean view, the agrarian landward view, and the dynamic ground plane itself. Perched safely above, flooding becomes a non-threatening event, a periodic change in the home's relationship with the ground. From the glass-enclosed bridges that connect the volumes, one can appreciate the dramatic spaces between the them, whether flooded in wet periods, or interconnected by flows of native plantings in the typical drier periods.

The composition of the volumes in the landscape is guided by program and the surrounding context. Each volume is oriented toward an ocean or a pastoral view according to its use and requirements for access, seclusion, and daylight. Programmatically, pulling apart the spaces allowed for maximum privacy as four guest bedrooms are separated from the living areas and master suite. Communal spaces have flexibility to flow to the outdoors and extend onto elevated decks by means of full-height sliding glass doors.

The building's location, straddling the agrarian and coastal landscapes, inspired the articulation of the wood siding. The board and batten design is reminiscent of nearby vernacular structures while its two-layer composition allows for selective control over its opacity. At grade level the boards are omitted and the battens form an open screen to let floodwater flow through it per FEMA regulations. Above, overlapping boards and battens are opaque to mask neighboring houses from view. At the roof line, the battens are omitted to let light filter between the boards. The transitions between the varying opacities occur along horizontal datum lines that ring the towers, breaking up the verticality of the facades and referencing tide lines left by fluctuating water levels.

The language expressed by the exterior siding translates to the design of the interior spaces as well. The horizontal datum lines are visually transcribed onto the interior walls as material transitions for interior finishes and wall claddings. Wood clad walls at the first level transition into wainscoting and plastered walls at the upper floors. This visual link expresses the seamless connection between interior and exterior as one travels throughout the house.

By deliberately admitting the natural elements into the home, their fluctuations become part of the daily experience of the inhabitants. Thus, one is made more keenly aware of the environment and its ever-changing character.

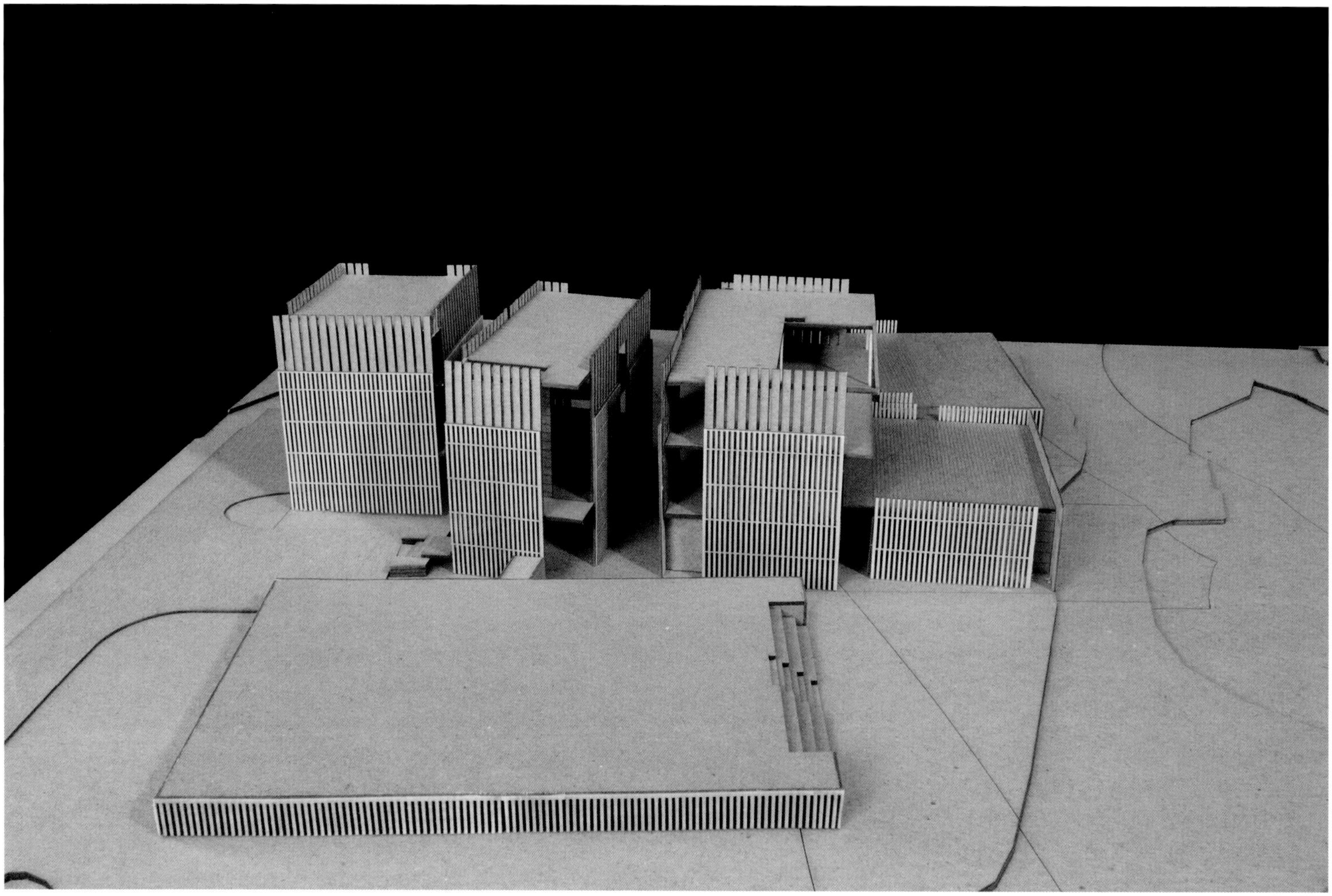

SITE PLAN

1. Main House
2. Elevated Lawn
3. Driveway
4. Parking
5. Lawn
6. Pool House
7. Pool
8. Deck

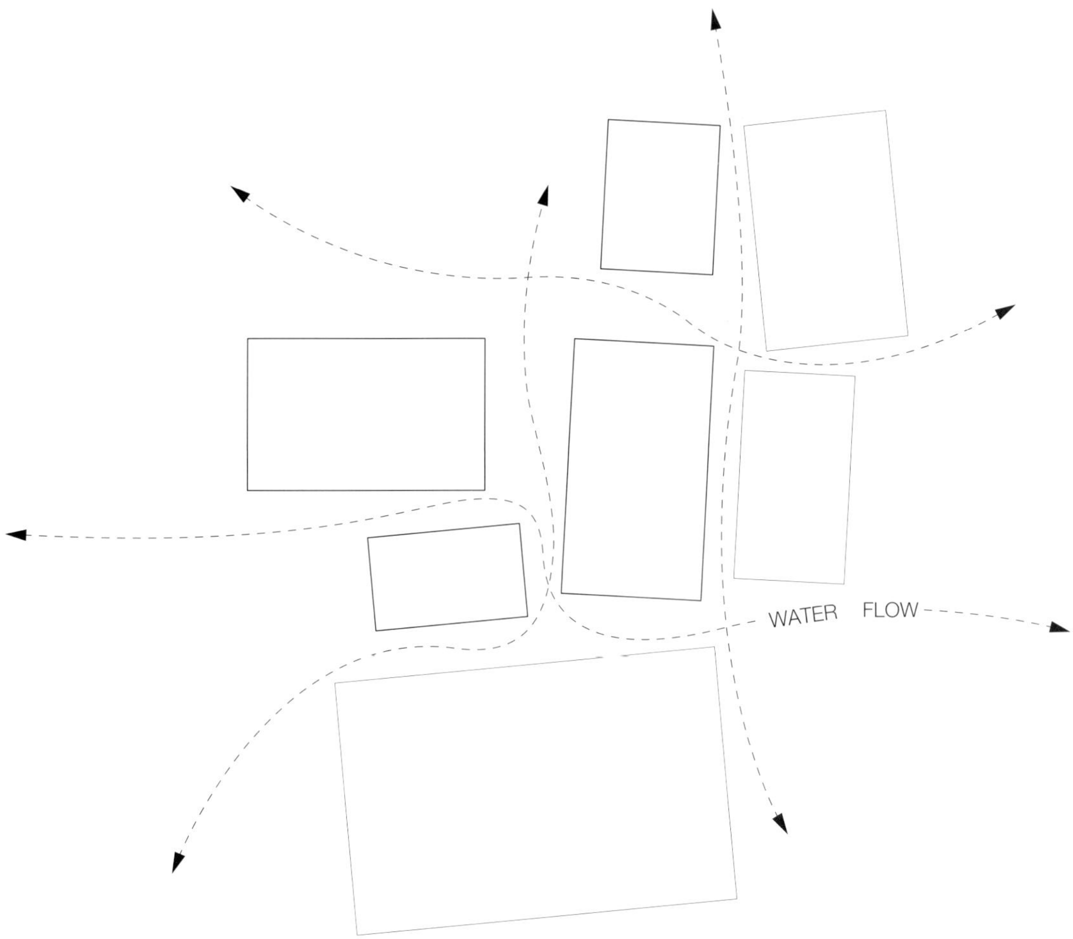

Subdivided and dispersed massing mitigates floodwater forces.

FIRST LEVEL PLAN

1. Entry
2. Stair
3. Elevator
4. Powder Room
5. Mudroom/Laundry
6. Bridge
7. Pantry
8. Kitchen
9. Dining
10. Living
11. Bedroom
12. Bath
13. Deck
14. Pool
15. Spa
16. Pool House
17. Pool Bath
18. Outdoor Shower

SECOND LEVEL PLAN

1. Bedroom
2. Bath
3. Bridge
4. Family Room
5. Stair
6. Elevator
7. Closet
8. Powder Room
9. Study
10. Deck

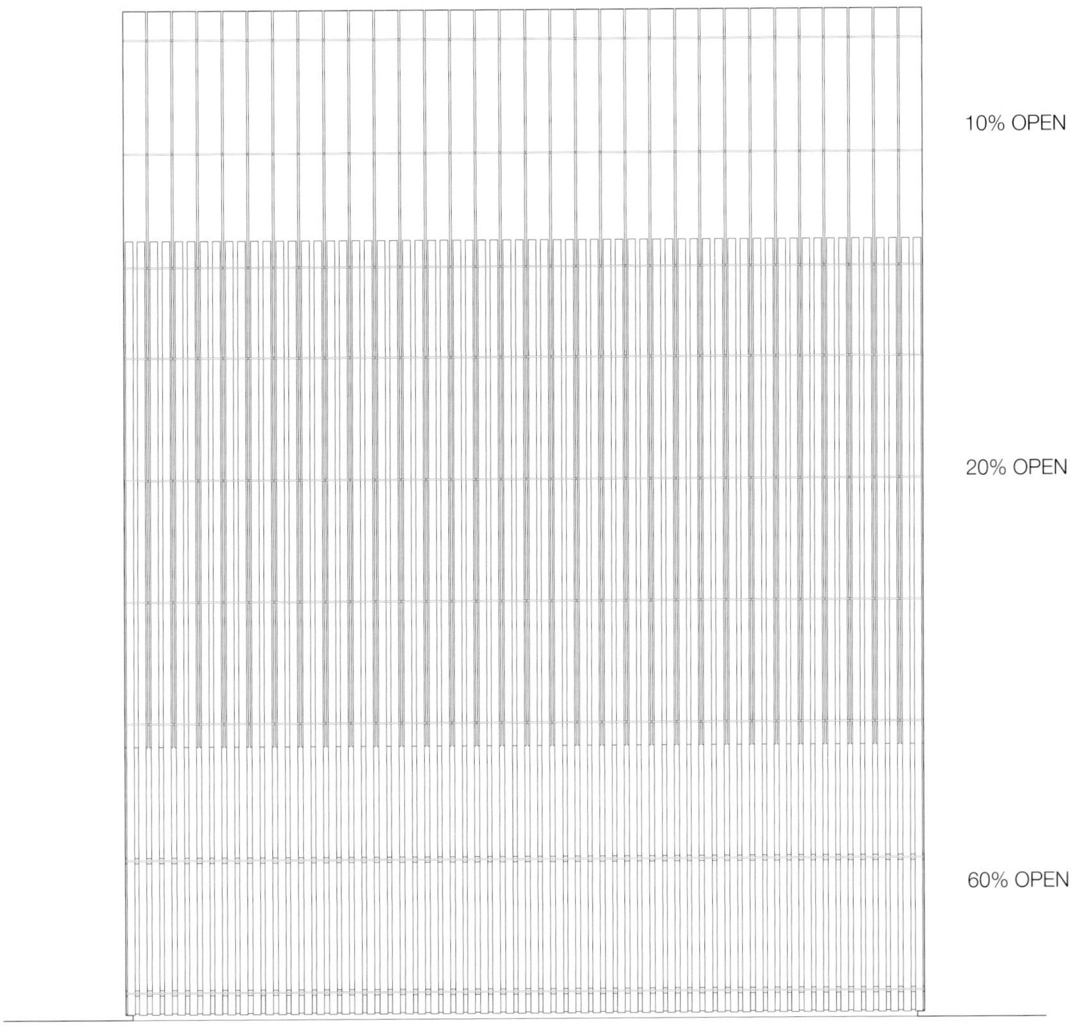

Siding porosity modulates to flood mitigation and privacy requirements.

Boards and battens adjust density along horizontal datum lines.
Opposite: Volumes spaced apart to allow the free passage of flood water.

Upper level datum line runs from exterior to interior.

WAINSCOTT

2020

At the end of the 19th century a private beach community was established from over 100 acres of coastal farmland. Large specimen trees, winding roads, early colonial architecture, agricultural buildings, and views of a large pond and the Atlantic Ocean create a bucolic setting. The proximity to the pond and ocean, however, brings with it the challenges of high ground water and flood risk. It was here that a family with a passion for art decided to build a home for their family, including future generations, and their art collection. They requested it to become a family heirloom. As such the home must anticipate the family's growth, providing space and privacy for guests, the couple's adult children, and their future grandchildren. It must be durable. It must also be elevated in anticipation of the future flood risk while preserving a connection to the landscape. Finally, the home must provide large openings to take advantage of the sweeping views, and at the same time limit direct sunlight on the art.

In response, the house was divided into three separate gabled structures dedicated to the couple and the two future families of their children. Each volume has it's own staircase to the unconnected 2nd floor spaces, which include bedrooms, lounge areas, laundry facilities, and kitchenettes. These separate self-sufficient volumes are connected on the main level by an art-filled circulation spine that opens to larger display spaces around the stairs. To provide indirect natural light, continuous clerestory windows along the spine allow diffused light from the north to filter through a carefully detailed exterior shingle screen. The openings modulate the light that enters, which is then reflected into the gallery space through oak ceiling coffers. The mechanical system is elevated above the spine to meet FEMA requirements and the supply and returns are concealed within the coffers. Artificial lighting is also integrated in the coffers, illuminating the art and backlighting the exterior screen. The continuous screen is a subtle change in the siding texture during the day, but highlighted when backlit at night, revealing on the exterior the continuous spine that unifies the individual volumes.

In each of the volumes, the stairwells double as larger art display areas and are naturally illuminated by northern light through bronze chimney light wells. The structure and cladding of each stair taper as they approach the floor, referencing the way light dissipates from the skylights above. The final art display area is the most dramatic: a day-lit glass cube that connects two of the gabled volumes to the third and serves as a sculpture gallery. A delicate cedar lattice wraps the glazing to filter the light and includes operable portions over sliding glass doors to allow for frequent rotation of the sculptures within. Lighting in this flexible space is mounted with magnets to allow for easy customization for each piece.

To ensure the home as an heirloom will endure, it is clad in durable materials that are applied in redundant layers. Cedar boards are installed like shingles in layers over a weathertight shell. Custom stainless clips hold the boards securely without penetrating them, allowing for them to expand and contract, or be easily replaced in the future.

The gallery spaces, circulation, lighting, and mechanical systems are interwoven into a spine that both ties the individual structures together, and symbolically ties the family together around their appreciation of art. The family will grow and change, as will their art, but the home will endure as a place of appreciation for both.

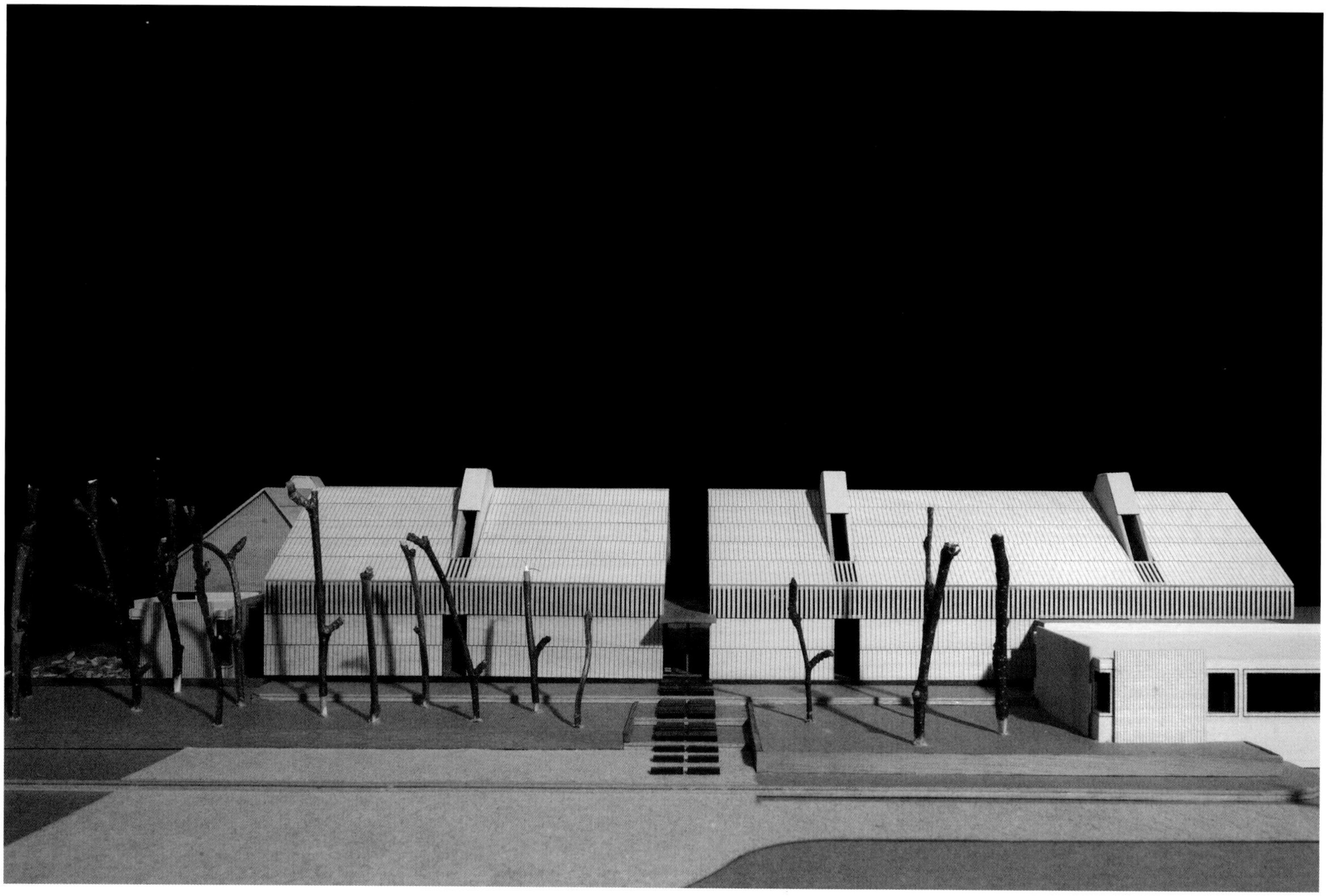

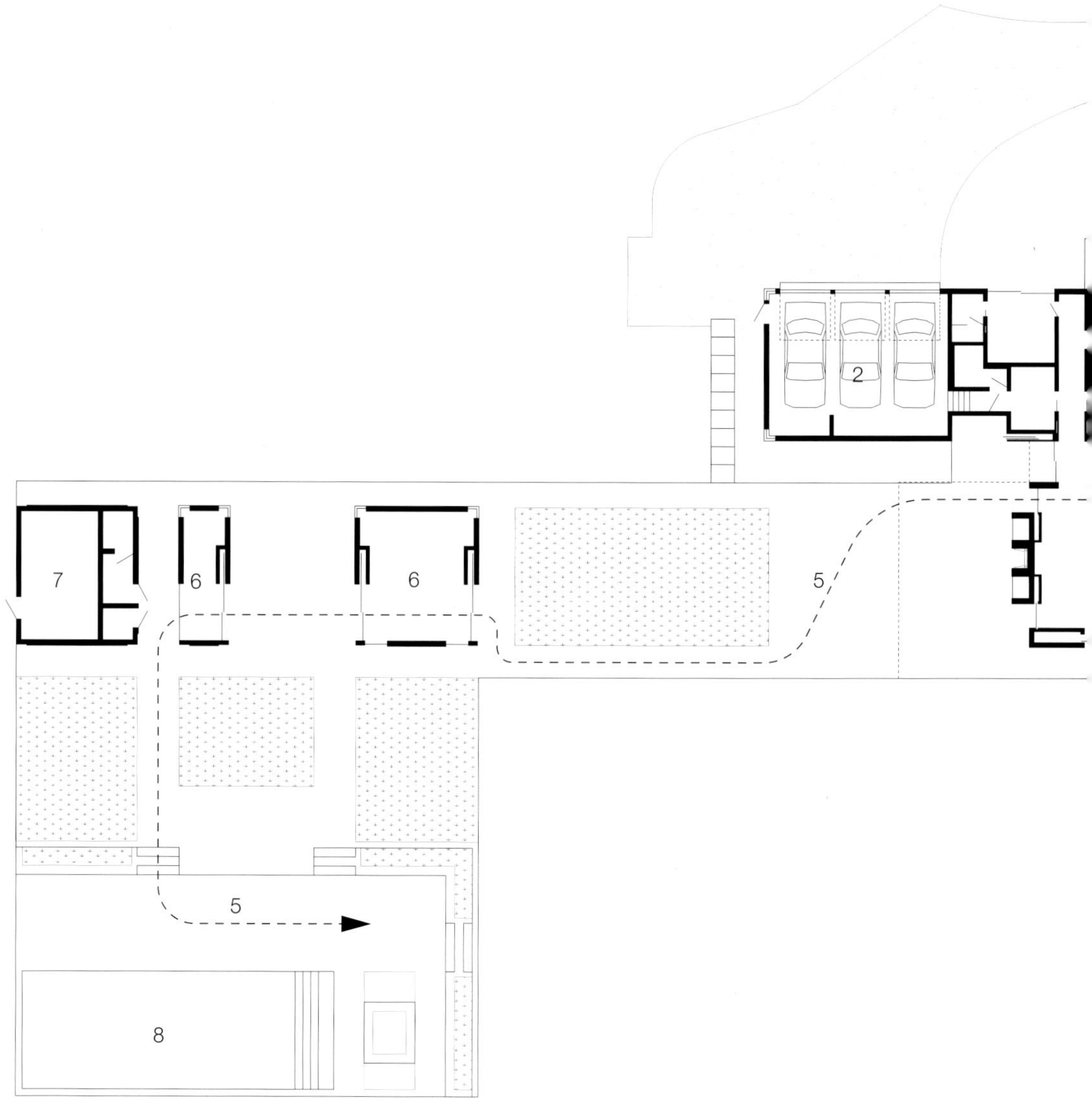

SITE PLAN

1. Driveway
2. Garage
3. Entry
4. House
5. Terrace
6. Pool House
7. Storage
8. Pool
9. Road

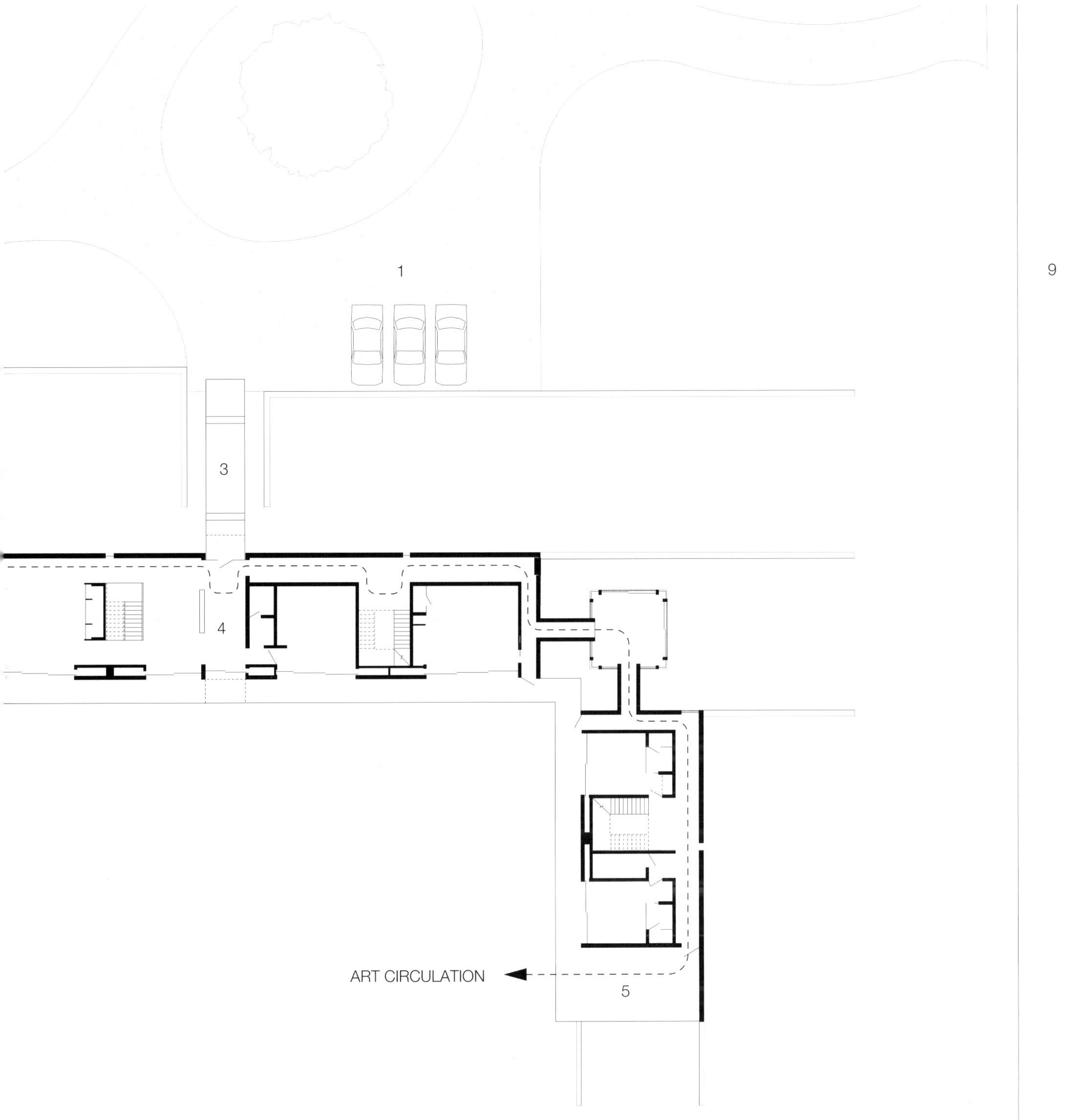
1
9
3
4
ART CIRCULATION
5

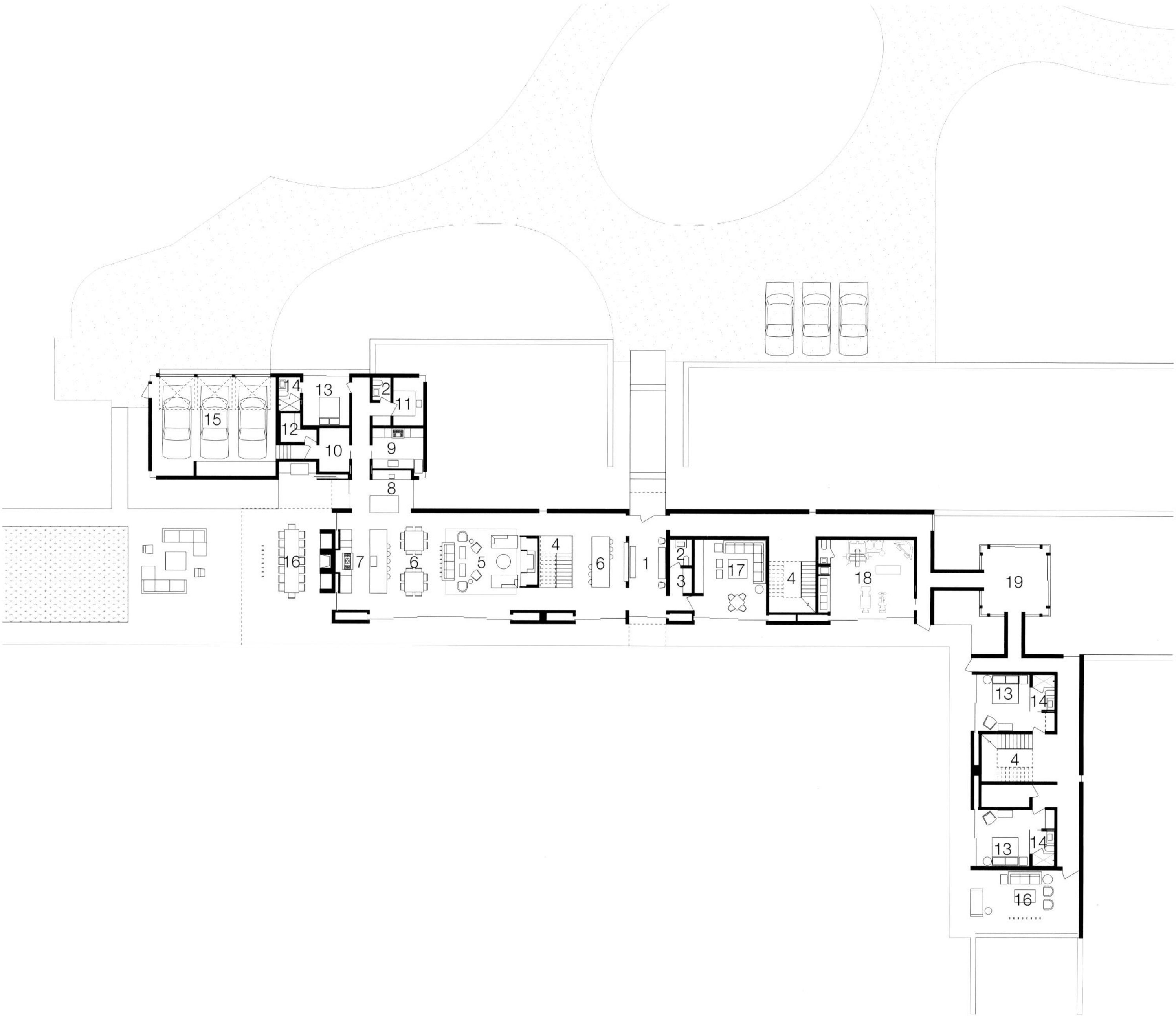

GROUND LEVEL PLAN

1. Entry
2. Powder Room
3. Closet
4. Stair
5. Living Room
6. Dining
7. Kitchen
8. Bar
9. Pantry
10. Mud Room
11. Laundry Room
12. Wine Room
13. Bedroom
14. Bath
15. Garage
16. Terrace
17. Media Room
18. Gym
19. Gallery

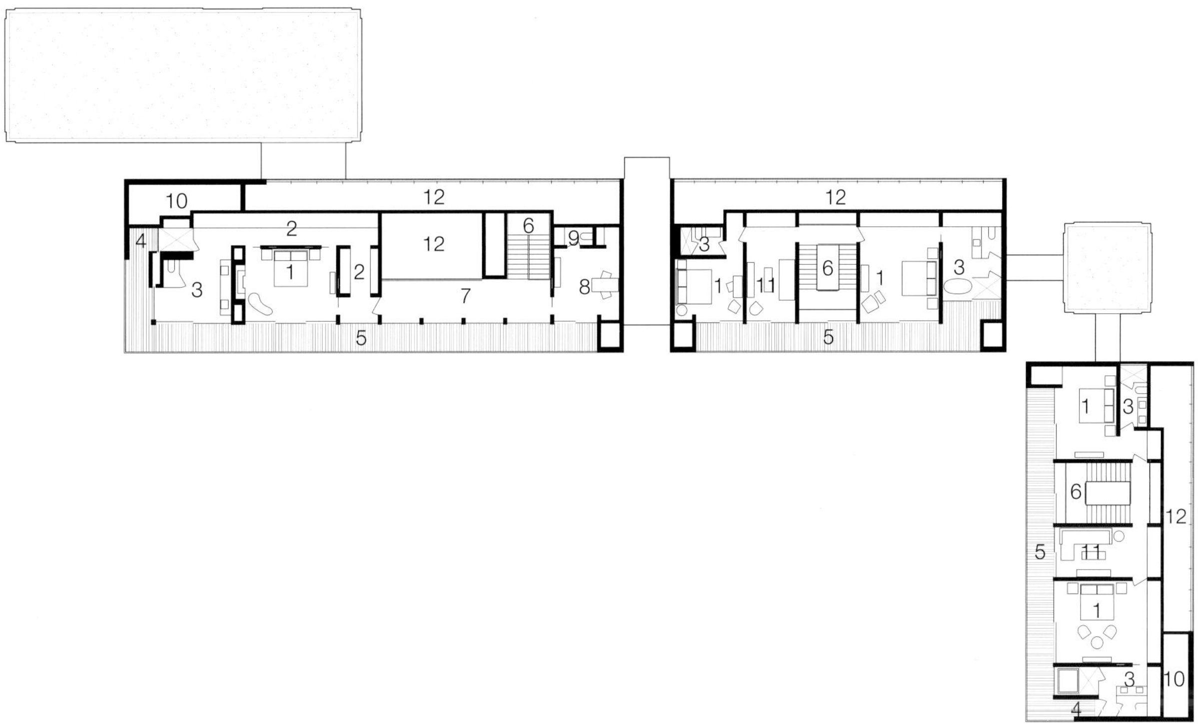

UPPER LEVEL PLAN

1. Bedroom
2. Closet
3. Bath
4. Outdoor Shower
5. Deck
6. Stair
7. Hall
8. Office
9. Powder Room
10. Mechanical
11. Common Room
12. Open to Below

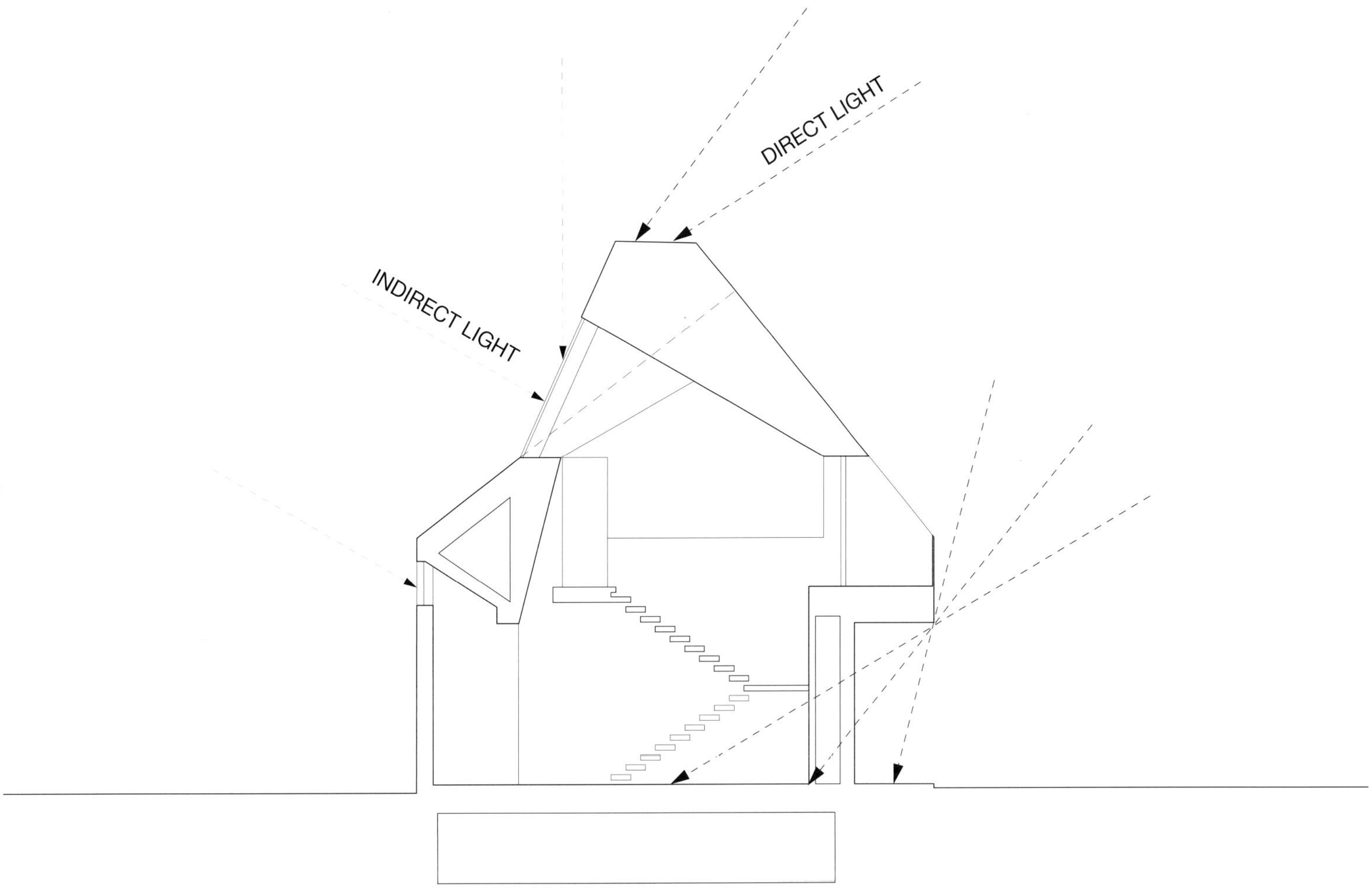

Roof and wall openings are choreographed in service of art preservation and display.

Art-filled circulatory spine continues through kitchen.

COINTREAU

Stairs break out from art spine to provide sculpture gallery.

Sculpture gallery at the intersection of the two axes.

NAPEAGUE

2020

In the early postwar period a community of twenty-five small, simple cottages was constructed among the rolling ocean dunes. This unpretentious enclave attracted fishermen, surfers, and beach lovers. In ensuing years the community became a gateway to an adjoining town, leading to increased traffic on the arterial roadway and railroad that pass along its northern edge. At the same time, improved environmental awareness brought attention to the risks of flooding from hurricanes that periodically inundate these lowlands. Tasked with replacing a weatherworn structure in this context, the challenge was to perpetuate the legacy of the beach cottage and its serenity of place, despite present-day disturbances.

Road and rail noise present the most pressing problem on this road-fronting lot. Though it may seem paradoxical at first, the new house is located closer to the road than its predecessor. This arrangement, with the structure stretched across the property, shields a large backyard from offending noise and opens it up to sunlight from the south. Walls facing the road are free of fenestration and extend into the side yards and above the roofline to enhance their shielding effect. An additional wall fragment in the front yard blocks sound at the entrance door, provides privacy, and defines the entry stoop. Research shows that mass optimizes a wall's sound-deadening properties, but conventional mass wall assemblies of stone or concrete are costly. Half-timber construction, common amongst the neighborhood's original cottages, inspired an economical alternative. Historically, half-timbering substituted a primitive timber frame infilled with sticks and clay (waddle and daub) for traditional masonry. These readily-available and easily worked materials created mass, which primarily provided protection from the elements. In this house, inexpensive, pliable sheets of mass-loaded vinyl, typically used to reduce sound transmission through floors, cover the building's framed exterior walls. The sheets fold together at their seams to form regularly spaced projecting ribs, not unlike the half-timbered frame, that set a cadence for the wood-siding panels' widths, the interior layout, and even the basis of light fixtures let into the walls' thickness.

The threat of flooding from storms presents a secondary problem. The property sits at a low elevation only steps from the ocean and inches above ground water. Current flood maps require the first floor of new construction to rise eight feet above the natural grade. To reconnect the elevated house interior with the landscape the front yard terrain is sculpted upward, restoring the property's original windswept dunes in the process. The backyard connection is reestablished through a series of descending decks, stadium seating, and steps that meet the swimming pool and the fire pit, which are raised out of the ground to avoid the water table and to form bench seating.

Drawing on the community's architectural heritage and half-timber construction with a new wall assembly, while sustainably engaging the environment via the dunescape's topography, the house reinvigorates the small enclave's sense of place and holds the restless outside world at bay.

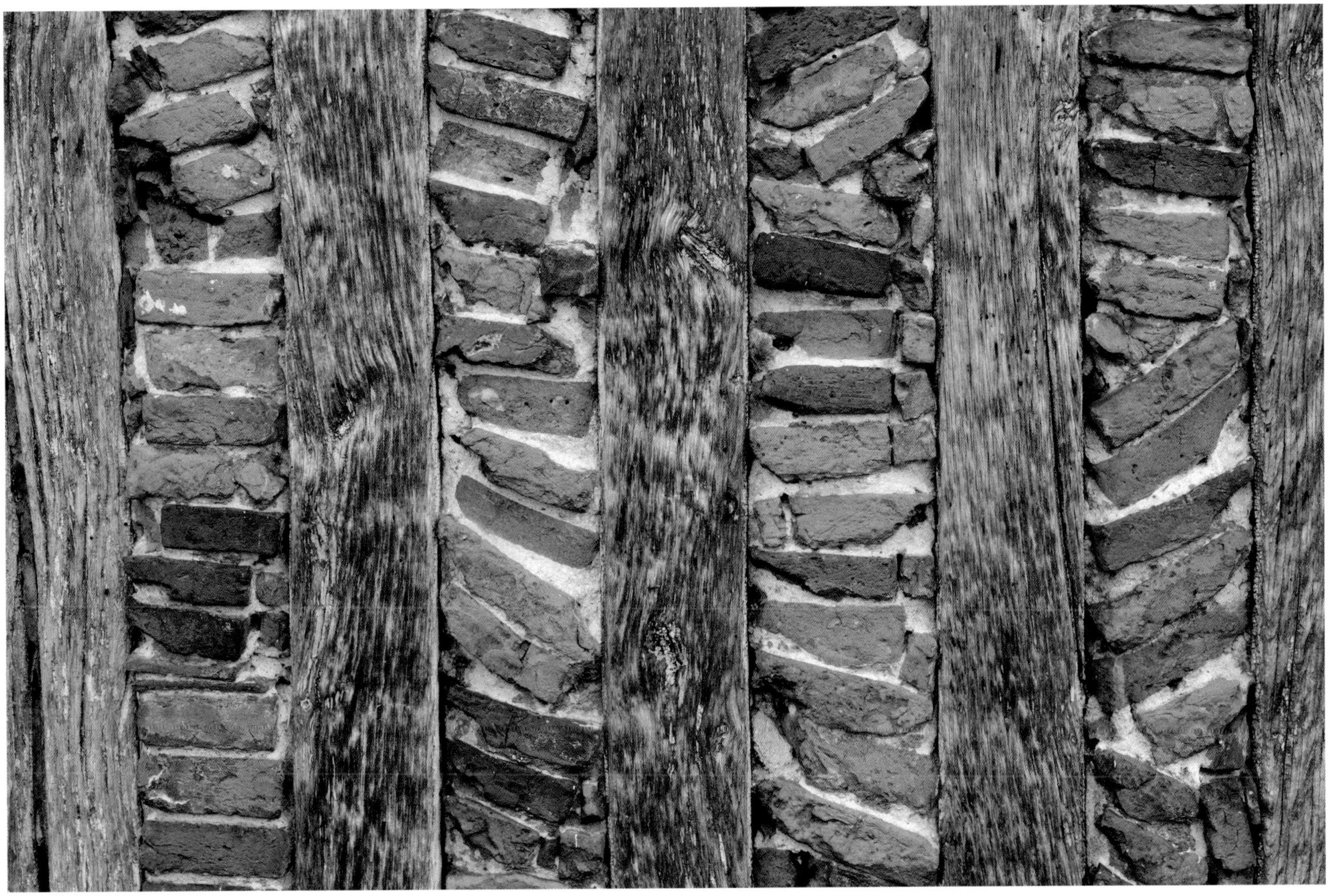

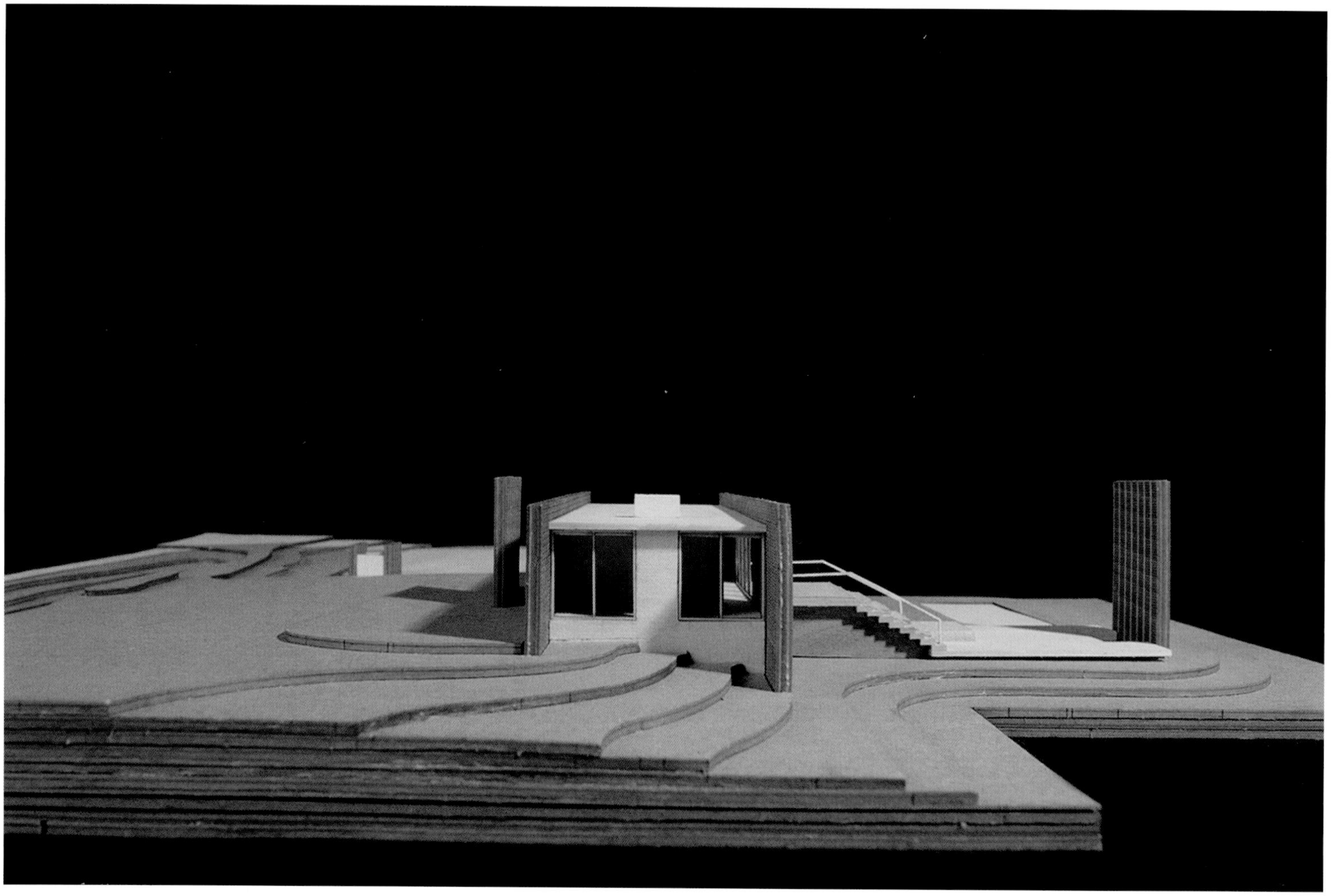

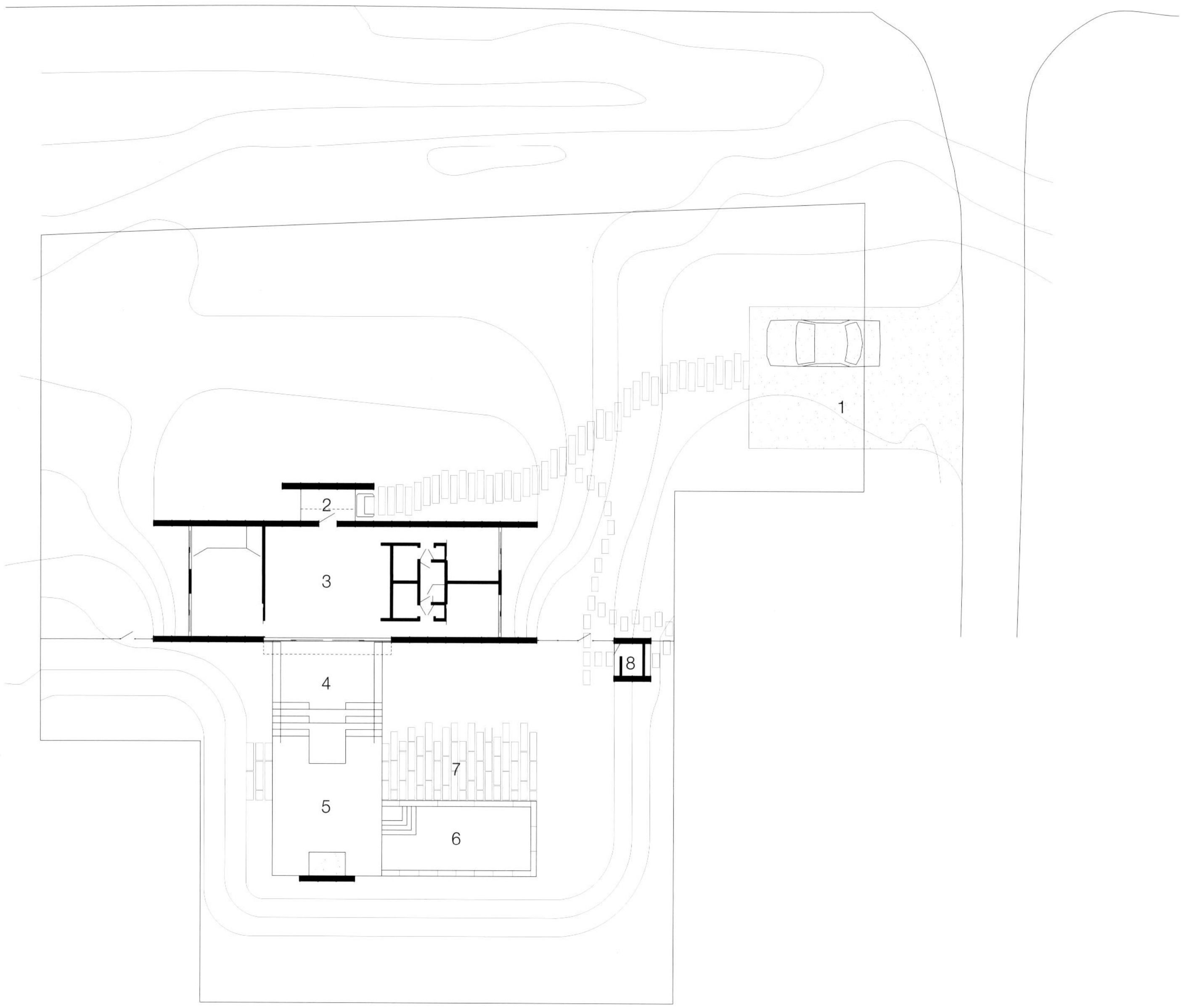

SITE PLAN

1. Driveway
2. Entry Deck
3. House
4. Outdoor Dining
5. Outdoor Living
6. Pool
7. Terrace
8. Outdoor Shower

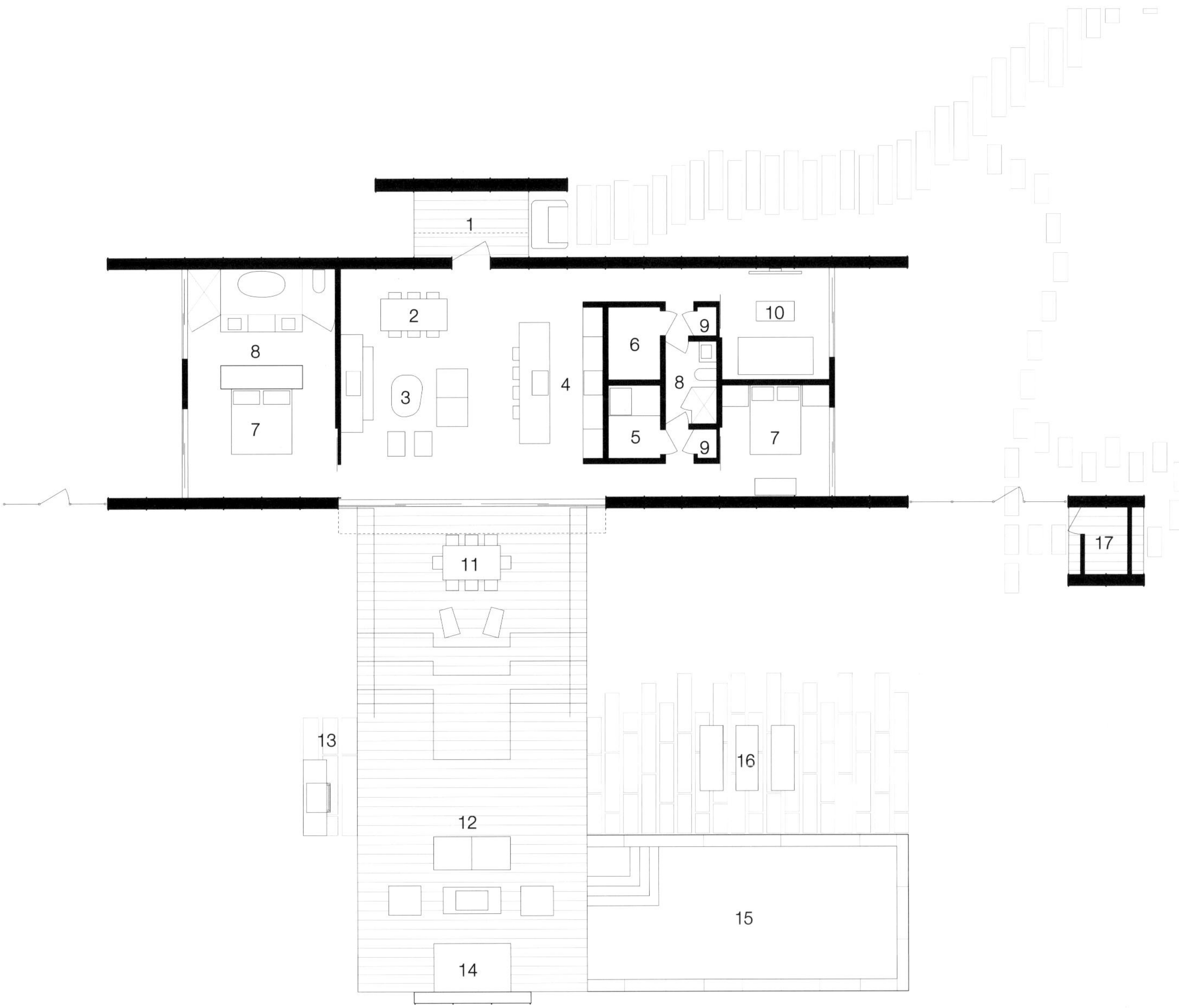

GROUND LEVEL PLAN

1. Entry
2. Dining
3. Living
4. Kitchen
5. Laundry
6. Mechanical
7. Bedroom
8. Bath
9. Closets
10. Den
11. Outdoor Dining
12. Outdoor Living
13. Grill
14. Fire Pit
15. Pool
16. Terrace
17. Outdoor Shower

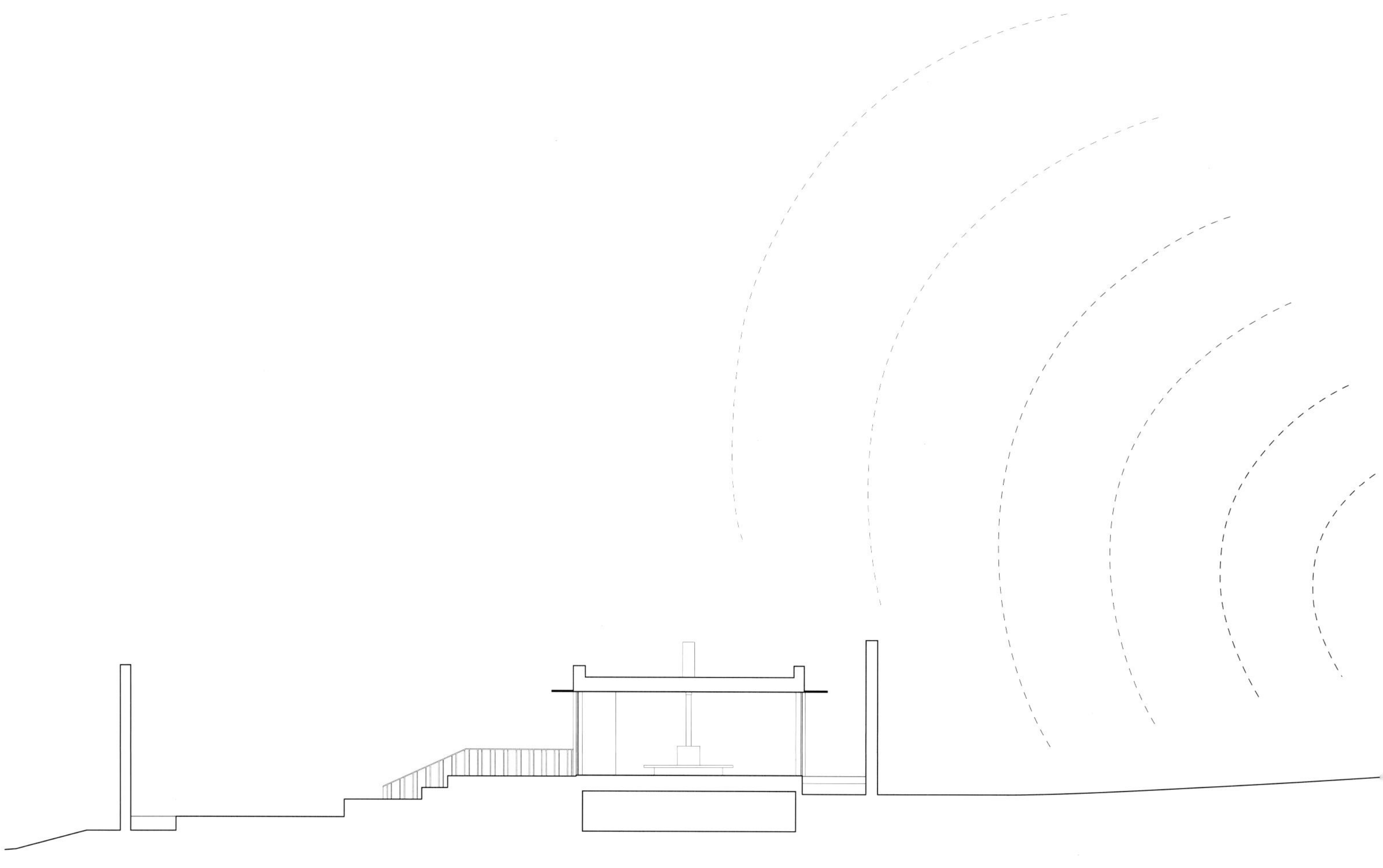

TRANSPORTATION NOISE

Mass loaded vinyl craned into place.

Expression of acoustic wall assembly on facade.

The exterior rib cadence is modified on the interior to create light fixtures.

LESLIE WILLIAMSON
BESPOKE HOME
Surf Shacks

STONY HILL

2020

This home for a young family is located in Amagansett, an early English and Dutch settlement on the East End of Long Island. The pastoral site, at the border between meadow and woodland, was first cleared by Native Americans as hunting grounds. Later it became the site of the first house built by a settler in 1680. Most significantly, it served as communal grazing pasture for the early settlers as the town was established alongside it. The meadow was divided into parcels with low stone walls and farmers rotated their livestock from one parcel to the next so as not to overgraze and damage any one area. This synergy among the land, livestock, and human intervention stabilized the landscape for generations. Recently, however, farming has declined as land values have increased, and grazing is no longer managing the meadow. Thus it is slowly transitioning to woodland and its connection to a significant piece of its history is fading.

The goal of the project was to reference the agrarian history of the site in the architecture and landscape design, principally by dividing the site into zones in a similar fashion to the original pasture parcels. In the same way that the parcels had different maturities of grasses due to the rotating grazing, the scale and density of the plantings in each zone were designed to vary based on modern needs: high grasses and shrubs provide a visual and acoustic buffer from the road, medium height grasses screen the house from the approach, and low grass and ground-cover open up views where appropriate. To emphasize the historic connections to the pasture, the planting zones that line the approach are elevated, bringing the grasses to eye level along the entry walk for a unique experience passing through them.

The massing of the house is broken up into smaller volumes, each of which relate to one of the landscape zones: public spaces, private spaces, and guest or service spaces. The interconnected gabled structures reference the connected barn vernacular precedent but are adapted for a modern experience. The steep roof pitches allow for ample 2nd floor space uninterrupted by collar ties. These traditional gable forms are subverted by cuts through the ridge to bring in natural light.

In the same way traditional forms are adapted, so too are historic materials transformed. The shingle siding common to the region is exaggerated in scale. In reference to the grasses of the pasture, traditional thatch siding is employed but it is packed neatly between the exposed exterior framing in a modern interpretation. The rhythm of the exterior framing is continued on the interior in the structure of the stair and the bath vanities. The exterior siding and paving are carried through the breezeways that connect the volumes of the house, further integrating the house with the site. Natural materials including oak, clay tiles, and plaster reinforce a connection to the landscape and a mood of warmth and comfort in the home. The gracious public spaces are each centered around oversized fireplaces to celebrate the family gathering together.

With its holistic approach to both architecture and landscape, the design translates the history of the place into a unique architectural vocabulary. In the process it preserves the pastoral character of the site, creates a record of the past, and enriches the family's home with deeper meaning.

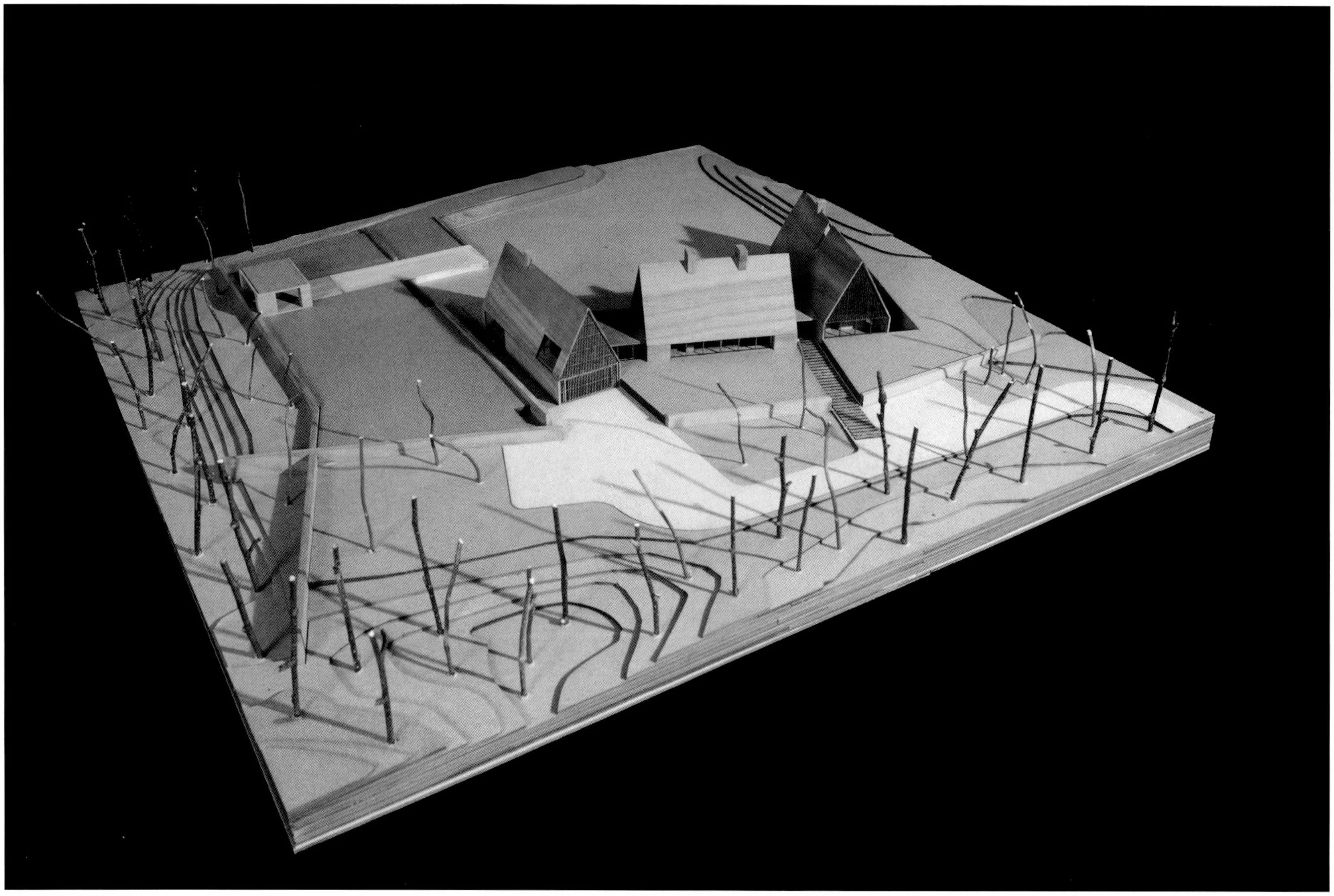

SITE PLAN

1. Driveway
2. Entry
3. House
4. Deck
5. Pergola
6. Pool

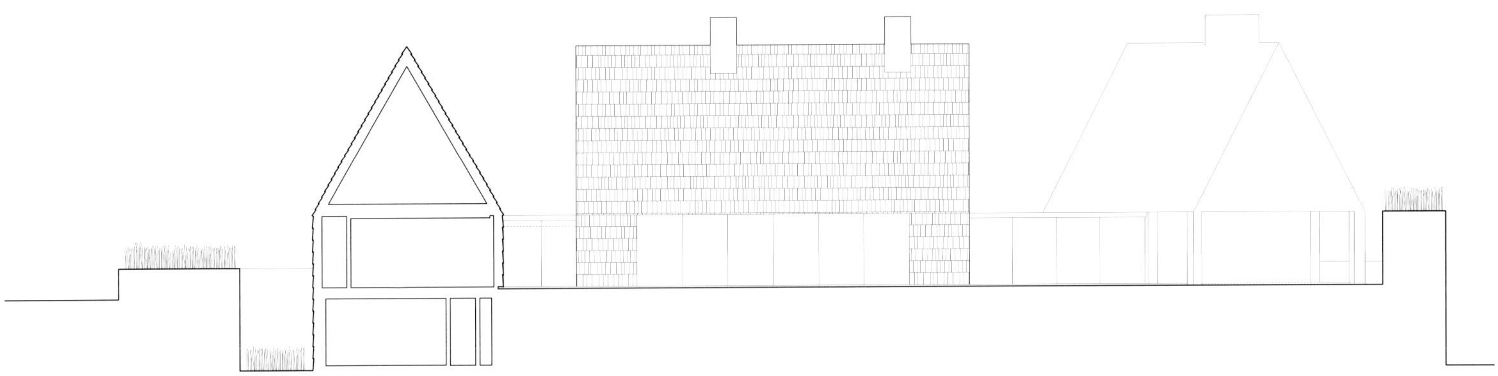

SECTION

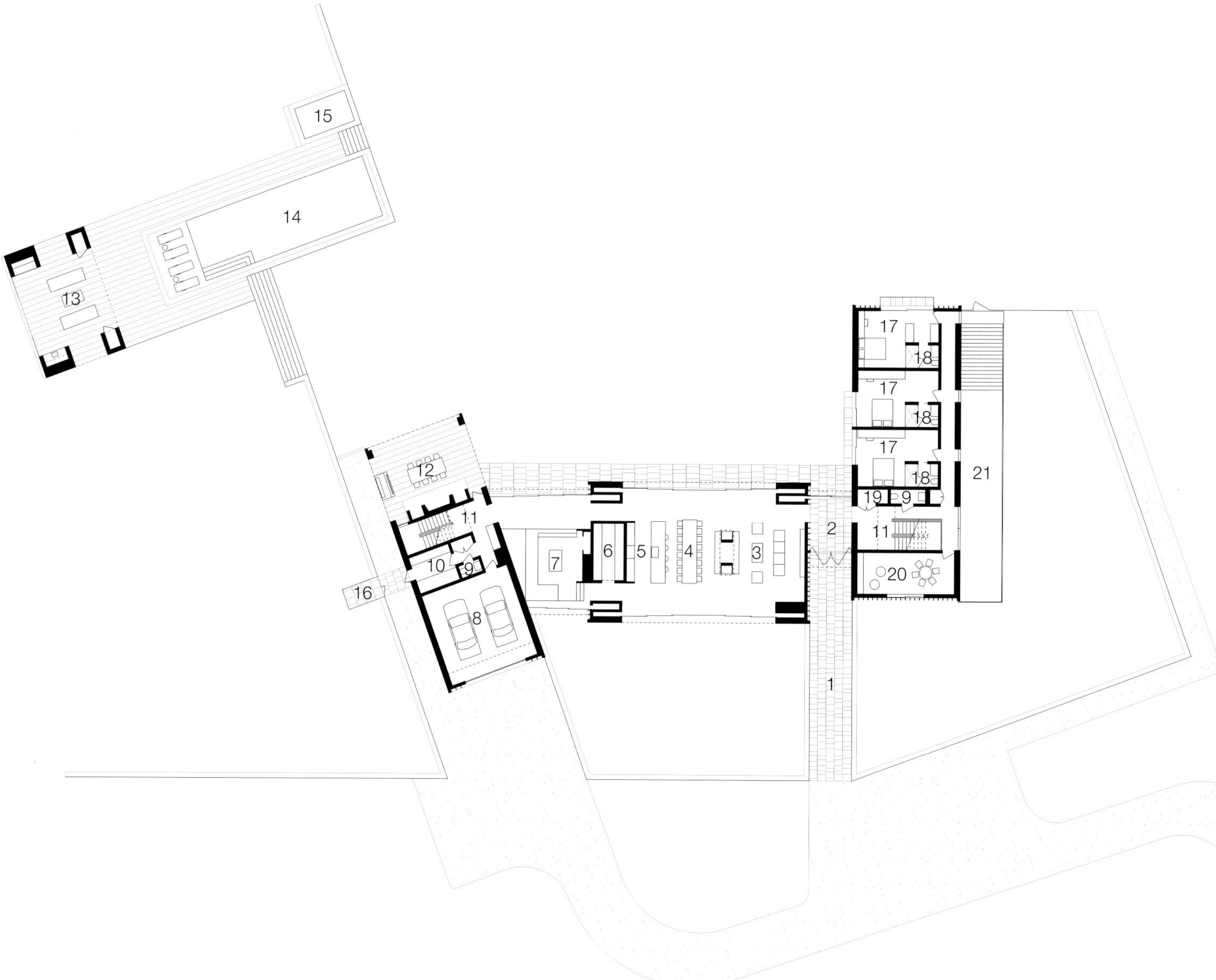

GROUND LEVEL PLAN

1. Entry Walk
2. Entry
3. Living
4. Dining
5. Kitchen
6. Pantry
7. Family Room
8. Garage
9. Powder Room
10. Mud Room
11. Stair
12. Outdoor Dining
13. Pergola
14. Pool
15. Spa
16. Outdoor Shower
17. Bedroom
18. Bath
19. Closet
20. Kid's Lounge
21. Light Well

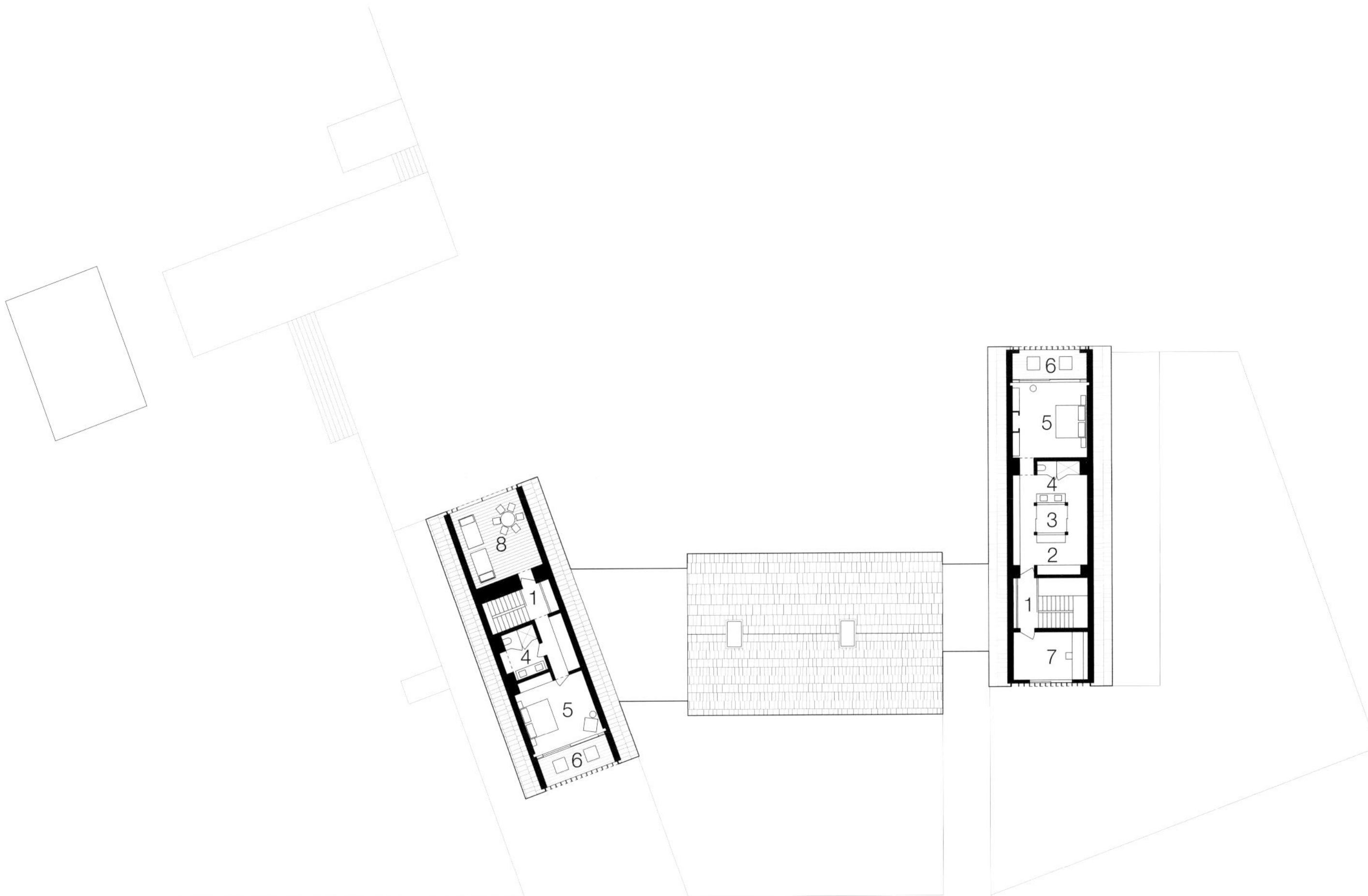

UPPER LEVEL PLAN

1. Stair
2. Closet
3. Outdoor Shower
4. Bath
5. Bedroom
6. Deck
7. Office
8. Screened Porch

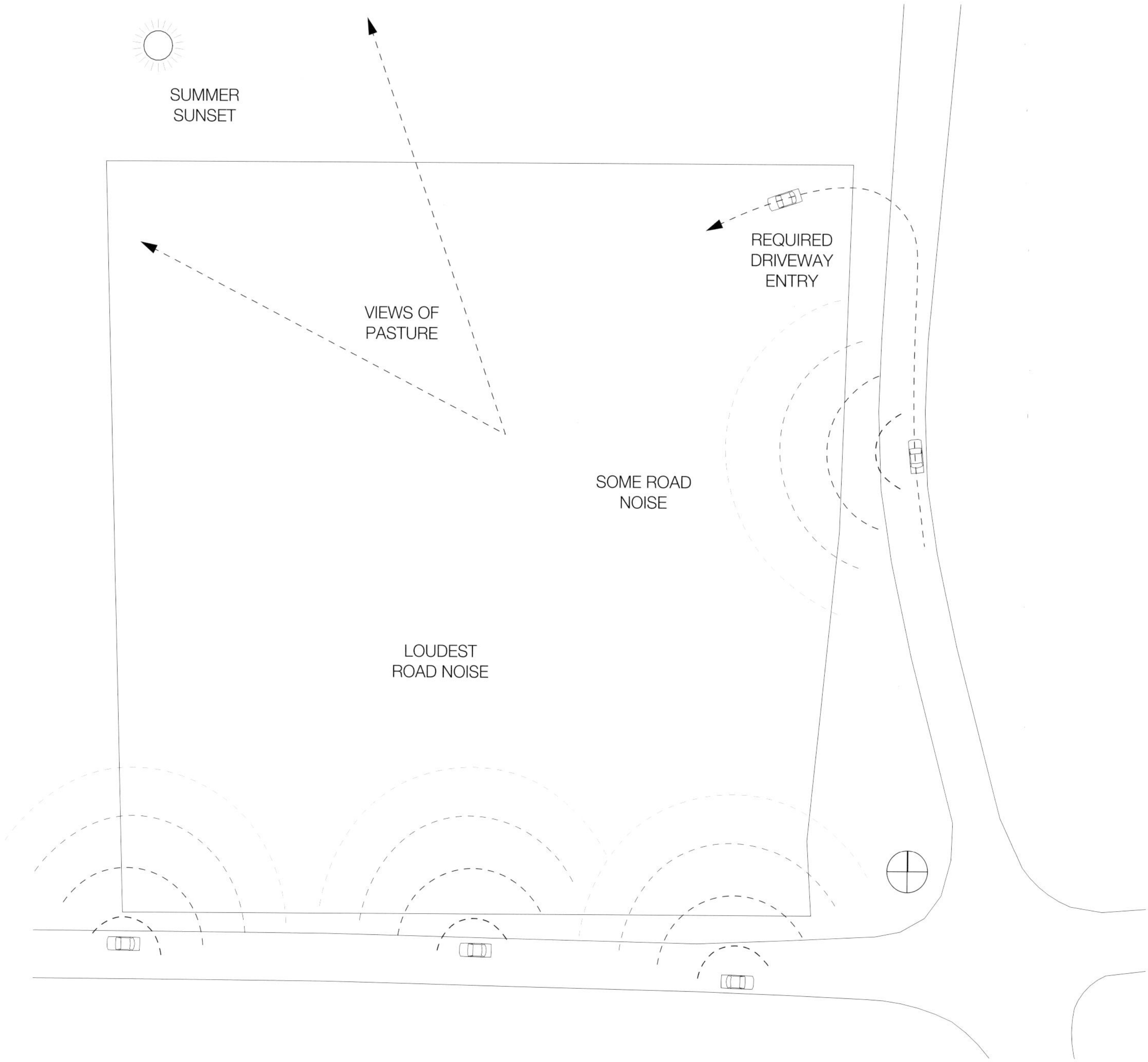

Road noise and views guide the arrangement of site and architectural massing.

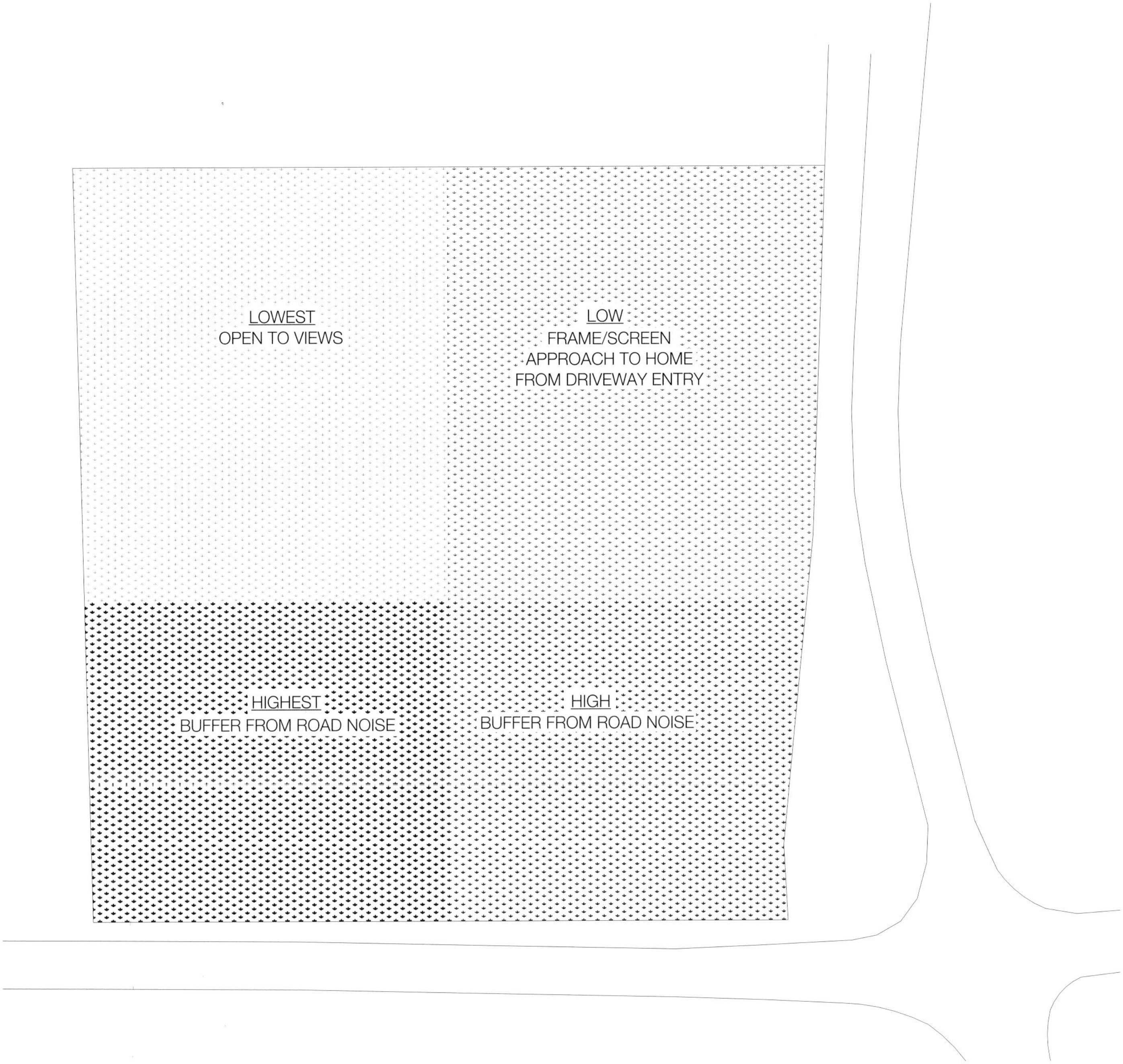

Landscape elements diagram.

Different grass species selected to peak throughout the seasons.

Exterior materials continue through breezeway.

Facade articulation continues on the interior.

SELECTED TIMELINE 2010-2022

BATES MASI + ARCHITECTS

2010 Residential Architect "Architects We Love"
2013 Interior Design Hall of Fame Inductee
2013 Best of Houzz – Design
2014 Cooper-Hewitt Design Nomination
2015 Cooper-Hewitt Design Nomination
2015 Ocean Home Top 50 Coastal Architects
2016 Best of Houzz – Design
2016 Cooper-Hewitt Design Nomination
2016 Ocean Home Top 50 Coastal Architects
2017 Best of Houzz – Design
2017 Wm. S. Marvin Hall of Fame Inductee
2017 Ocean Home Top 50 Coastal Architects
2018 Harry Bates – HC&G Innovator of the Year
2019 Ocean Home Top 50 Coastal Architects
2020 Ocean Home Top 50 Coastal Architects
2021 Best of Houzz – Design
2021 Ocean Home Top 50 Coastal Architects
2022 Luxe Gold List

SALT CAY *2010*

unbuilt

2010 AIA Peconic Merit Award

2010 ROBINS WAY

2011 AIA Long Island ArchiAward Commendation
2011 AIA Long Island ArchiAward Lighting Award
2011 AIA Peconic Juror's Award
2012 Interior Design Mag. Best of Year Honoree
2013 Watermark Award
2014 Remodeling Magazine Grand Award

QUAIL HILL *2010*

2010 AIA Peconic Honor Award
2010 AIA Long Island ArchiAward Commendation

2011 GENIUS LOCI

2011 Int'l Design Awards Gold Award
2011 CWC Residential Wood Design Award
2011 AIA Long Island ArchiAward
2011 AIA Peconic Honor Award
2012 AIA NY State Citation Award
2012 Architectural Record – Record House
2012 Residential Architect Mag. Design Award

SAM'S CREEK *2011*

2011 Int'l Design Awards Gold Award
2011 Int'l Design Awards Architecture of the Year
2012 Interior Design Mag. Best of Year Winner
2012 AIA NY State Award of Merit
2012 Metal Mag. Awards Honorable Mention
2013 Watermark Award

2012 TWENTY SEVEN

unbuilt

SAGAPONACK *2012*

2012 Int'l Design Awards 1st Place
2013 Interior Design Best of Year Honoree
2013 AIA Peconic Merit Award
2013 AIA Long Island ArchiAward
2013 Builder's Choice Custom Home Award
2013 AIA NY State Citation Award
2013 Residential Architect Mag. Merit Award
2013 Architectural Record – Record Bath
2014 Watermark Award

2012 FAR POND

2013 AIA Long Island Best of the Best
2013 AIA Long Island ArchiAward
2013 HC&G Innovation Award – Kitchen Design
2014 Remodeling Best of the Year Design Award
2014 Watermark Award
2014 Architectural Record – Record Kitchen

432 PARK *2012*

in progress

2013 NORTHWEST HARBOR

2008 AIA NY State Award of Merit
2008 AIA Peconic Merit Award
2013 Canadian Wood Council Award
2014 Int'l Design Awards Honorable Mention

MOTHERSILL *2013*

2011 AIA Peconic Merit Award
2013 Interior Design Mag. Best of Year Winner
2013 AIA Peconic Honor Award
2013 AIA Long Island ArchiAward
2014 AIA NY State Merit Award
2014 Int'l Design Awards Gold Award
2014 HC&G Innovation Award – Architecture
2014 Builder's Choice Custom Home Award
2015 Best on Archilovers

2013 PIERSON'S WAY

2014 Residential Architect Mag. Design Award
2014 Int'l Design Awards Silver Award
2014 Int'l Design Awards Honorable Mention
2014 Builder's Choice Custom Home Award
2014 AIA Long Island ArchiAward Commendation
2014 AIA Peconic Juror's Award
2013-14 Sub-Zero/Wolf Regional Winner

STAR RANCH *2013*

unbuilt

2014 SEBONAC CREEK

unbuilt

TESSA NYC *2014*

2014 Interior Design Mag. Best of Year Honoree
2015 Best on Archilovers
2016 Metal Architecture Design Award

2014 ELIZABETH II

2014 AIA ArchiAward
2014 AIA Peconic Merit Award
2014 Wood Design & Building Citation Award
2015 Residential Architect Mag. Design Award
2015 AIA NY State Award of Excellence
2015 Builder's Choice and Custom Home Award
2015 Professional Builder Gold Award
2015 Interior Design Mag. Best of Year
2015 IDA Gold Award
2017 SARA NY Merit Award

BEACH HAMPTON *2014*

2018 East End Design Awards
2018 AIA Long Island ArchiAward

2015 AMAGANSETT DUNES

2015 AIA Long Island ArchiAward
2015 Architects Newspaper Best of Awards
2015 AIA Peconic Merit Award
2016 HC&G Innovation Award – Architecture
2016 Professional Builder Silver Award
2017 AIA QUAD State Honor Award

PROMISED LAND *2015*

2015 AIA Long Island ArchiAward
2015 AIA Peconic Honor Award
2016 Builder's Choice and Custom Home Award
2017 East End Design Award

2015 HITHER HILLS

132 NORTH MAIN *2016*

2008 AIA Peconic Merit Award
2008 US Green Building Council Award
2016 Wood Design & Building Merit Award
2017 East End Design Award
2017 Architects Newspaper Best of Awards
2017 Interior Design Mag. Best of Year
2017 AIA Peconic Honor Award
2018 AIA NY State Award of Merit
2018 AIA Long Island ArchiAWard Commendation

2016 GEORGICA CLOSE

2016-17 Sub-Zero/Wolf Regional Winner
2017 Interior Design Mag. Best of Year Award
2018 AIA Long Island ArchiAward Commendation
2018 AIA Peconic Award of Merit

ATLANTIC *2016*

2017 Professional Builder Silver Award
2017 Architectural Record – Record Kitchen
2017 AIA Long Island ArchiAward Commendation
2017 AIA Peconic Award of Merit
2020 AIA NY State Merit Award

2016 SAG HARBOR SANCTUARY

1810 Church conversion to residence, in progress
2016 Professional Builder Gold Award
2016 Interior Design Mag. Best of the Year Honoree

UNDERHILL *2017*

2015 IDA Silver Award
2015-16 Wood Design Honor Award
2016 NYC&G Innovation Award
2016 AIA NY State Award of Merit
2016 AIA Peconic Award of Merit
2016 AIA Long Island ArchiAward Commendation
2016 Residential Architect Mag. Design Award
2016 Architects Newspaper Best of Awards
2017 Architectural Record – Record House
2018 AIA Housing Award

2017 GEORGICA COVE

2019 Residential Architect Design Award Citation
2019 AIA Housing Award
2018 Architecture MasterPrize
2018 AIA NY State Honor Award
2018 Builder's Choice Custom Home Award
2018 American Architecture Award
2018 Luxe RED Design Award – Regional
2017 Wood Design & Building Honor Award
2017 AIA Peconic Award of Merit
2017 AIA Long Island ArchiAward Commendation

ACTON COVE *2017*

2018 AIA Maryland Honor Award
2018 AIA Long Island ArchiAward Commendation
2018 AIA Chesapeake Bay Honor Award
2018 Interior Design Mag. Best of Year Award
2019 American Architecture Award
2020 AIA Peconic Award of Merit
2020 Builder's Choice and Custom Home Award

2018 SAGG FARM

2019 Wood Design & Building Award of Merit
2020 Residential Architect Design Award
2020 AIA NY State Honor Award
2021 AIA Peconic Honor Award
2021 RD Architecture Awards – Honor Award
2022 AIA Long Island AchiAward of Excellence

KIHT'HAN *2018*

2019 Professional Builder Gold Award
2019 Luxe RED Design Award – Regional
2019 AIA Tri-State Design Award
2019 AIA Long Island ArchiAward Commendation
2019 Interior Design Mag. Best of the Year Honoree
2019 Wood Design & Building Merit Award
2020 AIA Peconic Honor Award

2019 FAIRFIELD POND

unbuilt

PALISADES 2019

unbuilt

2019 ASSET

2020 Metal Architecture Design Award
2020 Architectural Record – Record Interiors
2020 NYCxDesign Award – Small Restaurant
2020 AIANY Merit Award
2020 AIA National Photography Competition
2020 Architects Newspaper Best of Design Award
2020 AIA Long Island ArchiAward Honor Award
2020 AIA NY State Honor Award
2021 AIA Peconic Honor Award

MILESTONE *2019*

2020 AIA Long Island ArchiAward Commendation
2021 Atas Project of the Year – Interiors
2021 Atas Project of the Year – Residential Walls
2021 AIA NY State Merit Award
2021 AIA Tri-State Merit Award
2021 MCN Project Excellence Award

2020 WAINSCOTT

2021 AIA NY State Honor Award
2022 Interior Design Mag. Best of Year Award

SIGNAL HILL *2020*

2022 AIA Long Island AchiAward of Excellence
2022 AIA NY State Merit Award

2020 MECOX

WEST COAST *2020*

2020 STONY HILL

2021 Architectural Record – Record House
2021 AIA NY State Merit Award
2021 AIA Tri-State Honor Award
2021 AIA Long Island ArchiAward Commendation
2021 Interior Design Mag. Best of Year Award
2022 Residential Design Honor Award
2022 AIA Peconic Honor Award
2022 Luxe RED Design Award

NAPEAGUE *2020*

2021 Builder's Choice Custom Home Award
2021 AIA Long Island ArchiAward of Excellence
2022 AIA Peconic Merit Award

2021 THREE MILE HARBOR

NAVY BEACH *2022*

2022 MORRIS COVE

SHINNECOCK *2022*

in progress

2022 QUOGUE CREEK

in progress

SANDS POINT *2022*
in progress

2022 WALKING DUNES
in progress

MOHEGAN TRAIL *2022*
in progress

2022 PAYNE'S CREEK
in progress

SHADMOOR *2022*
in progress

2022 VILLA V
in progress

HITHER WOODS *2022*
in progress

2022 BRIAR PATCH
in progress

TAFT *2022*
in progress

2022 HATCHERY
in progress

HARBORVIEW *2022*
in progress

2022 INDIAN WELLS
in progress

HEADLAND BLUFF *2022*
in progress

2022 WILL CURL
in progress

PRESIDENT'S BEACH *2022*
in progress

2022 SUMMER CROSSING
in progress

CREDITS

PROMISED LAND
Amagansett, NY
2015

Photographer: Bates Masi + Architects
Contractor: K. Romeo Inc
Structural Engineer: Steven L. Maresca
Furnishings: Elizabeth Bolognino Interiors
Landscape Design: Bates Masi + Architects
Contributors: Harry Bates, Paul Masi, Doug Farrell

ATLANTIC
Amagansett, NY
2016

Photographer: Bates Masi + Architects
Contractor: K. Romeo Inc
Structural Engineer: Steven L. Maresca
Furnishings: Bates Masi + Architects
Landscape Design: Bates Masi + Architects
Contributors: Harry Bates, Paul Masi, Danielle Caylor Farrell

GEORGICA COVE
East Hampton, NY
2017

Photographer: Bates Masi + Architects
Contractor: John Hummel & Associates Custom Builders
Structural Engineer: Steven L. Maresca
Landscape Architect: J. Medoza Gardens
Furnishings: Erica Millar Interior Design
Contributors: Paul Masi, Daniel Widlowski, Jack Booton, Adam Jordan

UNDERHILL
Matinecock, NY
2017

Photographer: Michael Moran
Contractor: Qualico Contracting Corp.
Structural Engineer: Steven L. Maresca
Landscape Architect: TL Studio
Contributors: Harry Bates, Paul Masi, Katherine Dalene Weil, Emily Ko Smith

ACTON COVE
Annapolis, MD
2017

Photographer: Michael Moran
Contractor: Pyramid Builders
Structural Engineer: 1200 Architectural Engineers PLLC
Landscape Architect: Gregg Bleam Landscape Architect
Contributors: Paul Masi, Aaron Weil, Adam Jordan

SAGG FARM
Sagaponack, NY
2018

Photographer: Bates Masi + Architects
Contractor: Lettieri Construction
Structural Engineer: Steven L. Maresca
Contributors: Harry Bates, Paul Masi, Katherine Dalene Weil, Emily Ko Smith, Xiao Lin, Beau Durham

KIHT'HAN
Sagaponack, NY
2018

Photographer: Bates Masi + Architects
Contractor: K. Romeo Inc
Structural Engineer: Steven L. Maresca
Landscape Design: Bates Masi + Architects
Contributors: Paul Masi, Aaron Weil, Ryan Berry, Emily Ko Smith

WAINSCOTT
Wainscott, NY
2020

Photographer: Michael Moran
Contractor: Men at Work Construction
Structural Engineer: Steven L. Maresca
Landscape Architect: Perry Guillot Inc
Interiors: David Kleinberg Design Associates
Lighting Design: Orsman Design
Contributors: Paul Masi, Katherine Dalene Weil, Nick Darin, Nick Braaksma, Hung Fai Tang

NAPEAGUE
Amagansett, NY
2020

Photographer: Bates Masi + Architects
Contractor: Merit Builders
Structural Engineer: Steven L. Maresca
Landscape Design: Bates Masi + Architects
Contributors: Paul Masi, Aaron Zalneraitis, James Willis

STONY HILL
Amagansett, NY
2020

Photographer: Bates Masi + Architects
Contractor: John Hummel & Associates Custom Builders
Structural Engineer: Steven L. Maresca
Landscape Design: Bates Masi + Architects
Interiors: JL Hummel Interiors
Contributors: Paul Masi, Danielle Caylor Farrell, Greg Scherer

ORO
EDITIONS

Publishers of Architecture, Art, and Design
Gordon Goff: Publisher

www.oroeditions.com
info@oroeditions.com

Published by ORO Editions

Copyright © 2023 Bates Masi + Architects.

All rights reserved. No part of this book may be reproduced, stored in a retrieval system, or transmitted in any form or by any means, including electronic, mechanical, photocopying of microfilming, recording, or otherwise (except that copying permitted by Sections 107 and 108 of the U.S. Copyright Law and except by reviewers for the public press) without written permission from the publisher.

You must not circulate this book in any other binding or cover and you must impose this same condition on any acquirer.

Graphic Design: Bates Masi + Architects
Project Coordinator: Alana Leland

Edited by: Aaron Weil, Bates Masi + Architects
Project Manager: Jake Anderson

10 9 8 7 6 5 4 3 2 1 First Edition

Library of Congress data available upon request. World Rights: Available

ISBN: 978-1-954081-19-2

Color Separations and Printing: ORO Group Ltd.
Printed in China.

International Distribution: www.oroeditions.com/distribution

ORO Editions makes a continuous effort to minimize the overall carbon footprint of its publications. As part of this goal, ORO Editions, in association with Global ReLeaf, arranges to plant trees to replace those used in the manufacturing of the paper produced for its books. Global ReLeaf is an international campaign run by American Forests, one of the world's oldest nonprofit conservation organizations. Global ReLeaf is American Forests' education and action program that helps individuals, organizations, agencies, and corporations improve the local and global environment by planting and caring for trees.

bates
masi+
ARCHITECTS
www.batesmasi.com